A Violent Grace

"Dietrich Bonhoeffer defined 'cheap grace' as grace
without the cross. In these scalding pages,
Michael Card touched my heart with the love
of Christ crucified and led me to an
unprecedented appreciation of undeserved grace."

BRENNAN MANNING,
AUTHOR OF THE RAGAMUFFIN GOSPEL

"Every encounter I've had with Michael Card
has brought me closer to Jesus. I'm confident
that this book will do the same."

MAX LUCADO

"What Michael Card sings at this level I most need:
The inaudible strains of warm truth that fly from
heart to heart and nourish the soul where all too few
have fed. Loving God is hungry work and only those
who hunger enough can feed the rest of us.
Michael Card knows how to set such a table."

DR. CALVIN MILLER,
BEESON DIVINITY SCHOOL, SAMFORD UNIVERSITY

"Always the careful teacher, Michael Card draws
the church back to a much-needed look at
the suffering Savior. Like me, you will gaze
with astonished reverence at the One Who
endured such violence, then bow in humble
adoration, crying, 'Lord, make me more like You.'"

STEVE GREEN

A VIOLENT GRACE
Published by Multnomah Publishers, Inc.

© 2000 by Michael Card
International Standard Book Number: 1-57673-688-1

Design by Stephen Gardner
Illustrations by Gustave Doré

Scripture references are from
The Holy Bible, New International Version (NIV)
© 1973, 1978, 1984 by International Bible Society,
used by permission of Zondervan Publishing House.

Multnomah is a trademark of Multnomah Publishers, Inc.
and is registered in the U.S. Patent and Trademark Office.
The colophon is a trademark of Multnomah Publishers, Inc.

Printed in the United States of America

For information:
MULTNOMAH PUBLISHERS, INC.
POST OFFICE BOX 1720
SISTERS, OREGON 97759

Library of Congress Cataloging-in-Publication Data
Card, Michael, 1957–
A violent grace / by Michael Card.
   p. cm.
ISBN 1-57673-688-1
1. Jesus Christ—Passion. I. Title
BT431 .C29 2000
232.96—dc21

00 01 02 03 04 05 06 — 10 9 8 7 6 5 4 3 2 1 0

A VIOLENT Grace

MICHAEL CARD

Multnomah®Publishers *Sisters, Oregon*

If you reject Him,

He answers you with tears.

If you wound Him,

He bleeds out cleansing.

If you kill Him, He dies to redeem.

If you bury Him,

He rises again to bring resurrection.

CHARLES SPURGEON

This book is dedicated, with deep admiration, to
Reverend R. L. Denson,
from whom the Lord took the cloak of violence
and replaced it with a garment of Grace.

Table of Contents

INTRODUCTION 13

1. HE WAS BORN TO DIE
   SO I COULD BE BORN TO NEW LIFE 19

2. HE SUFFERED TEMPTATION
   SO I CAN EXPERIENCE VICTORY 31

3. HE WAS BETRAYED
   SO I MIGHT KNOW HIS FAITHFULNESS 39

4. HE WAS ARRESTED AND BOUND
   SO I COULD BE RESCUED FROM BONDAGE 47

5. HE STOOD TRIAL ALONE
   SO I MIGHT HAVE AN ADVOCATE 53

6. HE WAS WOUNDED
   SO I COULD BE HEALED 63

7. HE ENDURED MOCKERY
   SO I COULD KNOW DIGNITY AND JOY 69

8. HE WAS CONDEMNED
   SO THE TRUTH COULD SET ME FREE 79

9. HE WAS CROWNED WITH THORNS
   SO I MIGHT CROWN HIM WITH PRAISE 87

10. HE WAS NAILED TO THE CROSS
    SO I MIGHT ESCAPE JUDGMENT 93

11. HE WAS STRETCHED OUT BETWEEN THIEVES
SO I COULD KNOW THE REACH OF LOVE 103

12. HE SUFFERED THIRST
SO I CAN DRINK LIVING WATER III

13. HE SAID, "IT IS FINISHED"
SO I COULD BEGIN MY WALK OF FAITH II7

14. HE WAS GOD'S LAMB, SLAIN
SO I COULD CLAIM HIS SACRIFICE AS MY OWN I25

15. HE WAS FORSAKEN BY THE FATHER
SO I WOULD NEVER BE REJECTED I33

16. HE CHOSE THE SHAME OF WEAKNESS
SO I CAN KNOW THE HOPE OF GLORY I4I

17. HE SHED HIS BLOOD
SO I CAN BE WHITE AS SNOW I49

18. HIS HEART WAS PIERCED
SO MINE COULD BE MADE WHOLE I55

19. HE DIED AND WAS BURIED
SO THE GRAVE COULD NOT HOLD ME I6I

20. HE ROSE AGAIN
SO I MIGHT EXPERIENCE ETERNAL LIFE I69

21. HE IS KNOWN BY HIS SCARS
SO I WILL TAKE UP MY CROSS AND FOLLOW HIM I77

Acknowledgments

I am grateful to Bill Jensen for suggesting the idea of *A Violent Grace* and for encouraging me to write the book for Multnomah Publishers. I would like to thank my editor, David Kopp, for going far beyond the call of duty to help me realize this project on paper. I am also grateful to Judith St. Pierre for so vigilantly and sensitively working through the final stages of the manuscript. Finally, I am indebted to Raymond Brown and his two fine volumes, *The Death of Jesus the Messiah,* which proved consistently helpful and authoritative for this work.

INTRODUCTION

Jesus is love made manifest.

CHARLES SPURGEON

I hold in my hand a small plastic replica of an ivory carving that I purchased at the British Museum. It is roughly three inches by two inches. Five characters are portrayed on the piece. First, on the far left, is Judas. He hangs from a small olive tree, his hands limp and lifeless. Barely discernible at his feet lies the money bag, its contents spilled out on the ground. Standing with her back to him is a woman I assume to be Mary, the mother of Jesus. She is looking down. Next to her is John, the apostle, also looking at the ground. He is making an uncertain gesture with his right hand. Is he reaching out for something or someone? To the far right, wearing a helmet and short tunic, is a soldier. He is the only character who seems to be alive. He is looking up. In one upraised hand he appears to be holding a knife.

The fourth character from the left is Jesus. He hangs from

the cross with a peaceful expression, His nakedness covered by a loincloth. Above His head the familiar Latin inscription reads "Rex Jud," an abbreviation for "King of the Jews."

What makes this artifact special is not its craftsmanship. It was not fashioned from some precious substance or overlaid with gold. As far as I know, it never belonged to anyone important or famous. What makes this carving important is the fact that it represents the first known depiction of the crucifixion of Jesus to come from the Christian community. Remarkably, it was not carved until A.D. 420, some 387 years after the event.

From early Christian art, from the catacombs for example, have come inscriptions, menorahs, anchors, Chi-Rhos, and the then secret but now familiar bumper sticker, *icthus*. We see Jesus depicted with His disciples, as the judge, at the raising of Lazarus, and, most often, as the Good Shepherd, with a lost lamb slung around His shoulders. Yet never, until this simple plaque, do we see Jesus depicted on the cross.

We can only speculate what the reason might be. We might be tempted to think that the early Christians were embarrassed by the cross. But in light of the fact that so many of them were being martyred for Christ, this doesn't seem likely. What makes the most sense to me is that for many years, the impact of the cross was still too graphic and gruesome. And still too personal. For many of them, crucifixion was less a fact of history than a contemporary horror. Many carried fresh memories of friends and family, some of whom had been used as human torches, hanging from crosses.

For a set of very different reasons, the cross seems to have disappeared from the Christian art and music of our own time. Worse, it has disappeared from many hearts and minds as well. Fewer and fewer of the churches I visit have crosses hanging behind or in front of the pulpit. Fewer songs sing of it. Fewer sermons celebrate it.

Particularly in American Christianity, the cross has become somewhat objectionable. Well-known pastors avoid referring to it in their sermons and on their TV programs because it is "too negative." Some contend that it is somehow "dysfunctional" to feel that we owe something to someone who sacrifices anything, much less himself, for us. Can't that become manipulation? Wouldn't it be better to respond to God for our own reasons rather than because we owe him something? Other people are put off by the violence the cross portrays. No question about it—the blood and gore and pain of the crucifixion would certainly get an R rating on the screen. Given the problem of violence in our society, why glamorize such things? Shouldn't we focus instead on the gentler side of the gospel?

From this greatest of negatives flow all the positives of our new life in Christ: from conflict, peace; from pain, healing; from death, life.

I must confess that my own ministry, which began with a singular focus on the cross of Christ, has slowly shifted towards more popular and palatable themes. I used to relish the criticism that I was "preaching and singing about the cross too much." In fact, the key verse for the first ten years of my ministry was: "I resolved to know nothing while I was with you except Jesus Christ and Him crucified" (1 Corinthians 2:2).

Lately, though, I've noticed that it seems to be easier to get things done by avoiding such criticism. My early critics were right: It's hard to sell songs about a crucified man. Better to sing, preach, and write about the positives—peace, prosperity, and easy grace. To a society obsessed with abundance and acceptance, the Good News minus the cross (which is no good news at all) does seem to keep the coffers and pews full.

What are we to do? Where are we to stand if we long to stand for Christ?

I believe that if we are to maintain biblical Christianity in the new century, we must refocus our attention on the cross. And not just as an idle, passing glance. We must live it and celebrate it. At a time when more Christians in the world are dying for Christ than at any time in the history of the faith, we must even be ready to die for it.

Fifty years ago, when some underground Christians in the church in Germany were asking many of the same questions about the cross, a man who would become a martyr asked, "How could something become cheap which cost God everything?" Dietrich Bonhoeffer gave his life to remind us that the cross of Christ will forever remain the center of our faith. From this greatest of negatives flow all the positives of our new life in Christ: from conflict, peace; from pain, healing; from death, life.

A friend of mine and his buddy were sitting together in a foxhole during the Korean War. Their patrol had been assigned to sweep for concealed mines. As they sat together, sharing a candy bar, an enemy hand grenade flew through the air and landed between them. Without hesitation, my friend's partner threw aside the last piece of candy bar and flung himself on the grenade. His courage saved my friend's life.

When I first heard that story, I thought, *I know someone who was died for.* Then the truth hit me: I was "died for," too. Jesus fell on the grenade, as it were, for me. He placed Himself in harm's way so I could be saved. The cross proves that you and I are valued and loved beyond our wildest imaginings—so much, in fact, that we were died for.

The purpose of this book is to help you see the cross for what it is: on the one hand, the scene of the violent execution of the Son of God and, on the other, the source of His limitless grace.

HE WAS BORN TO DIE
SO I COULD BE BORN TO NEW LIFE

> *Anyone who is hung on a tree
> is under God's curse.*
>
> DEUTERONOMY 21:23

*T*he sounds of the first Christmas….

The clip-clop of the donkey as Mary and Joseph enter the quiet streets of Bethlehem. The rustling of straw as they make their bed for the night. The music of angels over those lonely hills. And the cooing of a baby.

The sounds of that night are full of joy. Even the angels' announcement of Jesus' arrival roll out like hymns of grace—*Immanuel, Savior, a light for the Gentiles, the Son of the most High, glory…!* The notion of violence is nowhere to be found.

You and I would like to keep it that way. Who wants to ruin a story of such beauty and hope with even a hint of pain?

Certainly Mary and Joseph didn't. But when the proud parents took their newborn to the temple for His dedication, it was there. A hint. A scarlet thread. After Simeon, an elderly, devout temple attendant, blessed the child, he turned to Mary and said, "A sword will pierce your own soul" (Luke 2:35). His words were unexpected. How could Mary have understood them? How could she not have been frightened?

Simeon's words were the first faint whisper that the grace baby Jesus had come to lavish on a fallen world would be bought at a terrible price. Within months, the scarlet thread turned to blood in the streets. Herod's soldiers swept through Bethlehem and the surrounding towns, slaughtering all male infants under two years old. Cries of horror and disbelief rose from the lips of bereft mothers and fathers, brothers and sisters and grandparents. Those, too, are the sounds of Christmas.

Only Jesus understood. During His ministry, Jesus often spoke of hard-to-grasp paradoxes: He was both king and suffering servant; both healer and wounded one; both everlasting God and crucified outcast.

Once when Jesus told His disciples that He would suffer and die, Peter cried out, "Never, Lord! This shall never happen to you!" (Matthew 16:22). No doubt he spoke for the Twelve. If I had walked with Jesus then, Peter would have spoken for me as well. But Jesus sharply rebuked Peter. He would not be turned aside from His mission. Luke wrote, "As the time approached for him to be taken up to heaven, Jesus resolutely set out for Jerusalem" (Luke 9:51).

Every day of His adult life stretched out ahead of Him like a narrow road. More than anyone else He knew that the script for His life had already been written across the pages of the Old Testament. As He made His way toward Golgotha, with every step He knew—detail for detail, agony by agony—how it would end and what it would cost.

∽✑

Many Christians are surprised to learn that there is more detail about the crucifixion of Jesus in the Old Testament than in the New. In the New Testament, the actual crucifixion is usually described within the confines of a single verse: "They crucified him" (Mark 15:24; Matthew 27:35; Luke 23:33; John 19:18). The Gospels, for example, don't tell us about the piercing of Jesus' hands and feet. We see Him pointing to those wounds only after the Resurrection. On the other hand, Old Testament predictions about the crucifixion of Jesus are numerous, and many of them are unsettling:

- *He will be rejected by his own people. (Isaiah 53:3)*
- *He will be betrayed by a friend. (Psalm 41:9)*
- *He will be sold for thirty pieces of silver. (Zechariah 11:12)*
- *He will be accused by false witnesses. (Psalm 35:11)*
- *He will be silent when accused. (Isaiah 53:7)*
- *He will be scorned and mocked. (Psalm 22:7)*
- *He will be spat upon. (Isaiah 50:6)*
- *He will be crucified with criminals. (Isaiah 53:12)*
- *Soldiers will gamble for his clothes. (Psalm 22:18)*
- *He will be given vinegar mixed with gall to drink. (Psalm 69:21)*
- *He will pray for his enemies. (Psalm 109:4)*
- *None of his bones will be broken. (Psalm 34:20)*
- *He will be buried in a rich man's tomb. (Isaiah 53:9)*

Yet these are only the factual details. As astonishing as they are, what I find even more remarkable is the Old Testament's account of Jesus' emotional and spiritual experience on the cross. King David and the prophet Isaiah wrote the most important prophetic passages some seven hundred to one thousand years before that joyful night in the stable or that dark day on Calvary.

In Psalm 22 David memorably captures the agony of the cross. I encourage you to take the time to read the entire psalm. But look with me now at a few high points:

> *My God, my God, why have you forsaken me?*
> *Why are you so far from saving me,*
> *so far from the words of my groaning?*
> *All who see me mock me; they hurl insults,*
> *shaking their heads:*
> *"He trusts in the LORD; let the LORD rescue him."*
>
> *I am poured out like water, and all my bones are out of joint.*
> *My heart has turned to wax; it has melted away within me.*
> *My strength is dried up like a potsherd,*
> *and my tongue sticks to the roof of my mouth;*
> *you lay me in the dust of death.*
> *Dogs have surrounded me;*
> *a band of evil men has encircled me,*
> *they have pierced my hands and my feet.*
> *I can count all my bones; people stare and gloat over me.*
> *They divide my garments among them*
> *and cast lots for my clothing.*

(PSALM 22:1, 7–8, 14–18)

In this anguished cry of an innocent man, we have a detailed account of Jesus' death—centuries before the torture of crucifixion was even invented! No wonder this psalm is quoted in the New Testament more than any other.

Some scholars believe that Jesus quoted the entire psalm on the cross and that the evangelists recorded only the first line. In Jesus' day if someone quoted the first line, everyone assumed that the entire psalm was meant. These scholars say that Jesus was moved to recite Scripture in order to give voice to the depths of His experience. People in torment, however, are unlikely to quote long passages. They groan and struggle to say anything coherently. As you would expect, all the words of Jesus from the cross that were recorded are short, gasping outbursts, as when Jesus cried, "My God, my God, why have you forsaken me?"

But was Jesus quoting David, or did David prophetically quote Jesus? What seems more likely to me—and even more amazing—is that it was, in fact, David who quoted Jesus. I believe David was granted the spiritual insight to enter into Jesus' experience: the abandonment (v. 1), the shame (vv. 7–8), the memories (vv. 9–10), the hope (vv. 19–20), and, finally, the praise (v. 23).

Other prophets experienced God's emotional life as well, most notably Jeremiah and Hosea, who were inwardly moved to feel His deep grief over wayward Israel. Later, Paul commended the same level of identification to all believers when he wrote, "I want to know Christ and the power of his resurrection and the fellowship of sharing in his sufferings, becoming like him in his death" (Philippians 3:10).

We find further evidence of David's identification with Jesus' trauma on the cross in Psalm 69. David compares his sufferings to the terror of sinking hopelessly into mud:

> *Save me, O God,*
> *for the waters have come up around my neck.*

I sink in the miry depths,
where there is no foothold.

(PSALM 69:1–2)

Further on in the psalm, there is more foreshadowing of Christ's suffering:

You know how I am scorned, disgraced and shamed;
all my enemies are before you.
Scorn has broken my heart and has left me helpless;
I looked for sympathy, but there was none,
for comforters, but I found none.
They put gall in my food
and gave me vinegar for my thirst.

(PSALM 69:19–21)

There is a terrible irony in David's musical notations, which preface these two prophetic psalms. Imagine hearing about bones being out of joint and a heart melting like wax to the sweet melody of "Doe of the Morning" (Psalm 22). Try to picture singing about slow suffocation by drowning in muck to the tune of "Lilies" (Psalm 69). As a musician, I think it adds to the emotional impact—like listening to the dinner music of the ship's string quartet as the mighty *Titanic* sinks into the sea.

Isaiah writes less intimately, but no less emotionally than David. In Isaiah 53 (see following sidebar), you'll notice that he is more of an onlooker—more of a prophetic eyewitness—than a participant. To describe the life and death of God's suffering servant, Isaiah begins with the tenderness of Jesus' childhood and the ordinariness of His life:

> *He grew up before him like a tender shoot,*
> *and like a root out of dry ground.*
> *He had no beauty or majesty to attract us to him,*
> *nothing in his appearance that we should desire him.*

> (ISAIAH 53:2)

But Isaiah, by the power of the Spirit, saw beyond outward appearances into the heart of Jesus' earthly experience:

> *He was despised and rejected by men,*
> *a man of sorrows, and familiar with suffering.*
> *Like one from whom men hide their faces*
> *he was despised, and we esteemed him not.*

> (ISAIAH 53:3)

Now hear the melancholy beauty in the prophet's familiar refrain. Let the majesty of God's redemptive plan sing in your own heart:

> *Surely he took up our infirmities*
> *and carried our sorrows,*
> *yet we considered him stricken by God,*
> *smitten by him and afflicted.*
> *But he was pierced for our transgressions,*
> *he was crushed for our iniquities;*
> *the punishment that brought us peace was upon him,*
> *and by his wounds we are healed.*

> (ISAIAH 53:4–5)

In this message from across the centuries, Isaiah tells us why Jesus—the innocent babe of Christmas—would be struck with infirmity, suffer affliction and piercing, and be wounded, crushed, and punished:

- *Because only by this unequal exchange could He pay the cost of my sin.*
- *Because only by this pain could He purchase my peace.*
- *Because only by this injury could He provide me with healing.*

Like David, Isaiah sees the ultimate prize, first for the risen Savior, and then for us, his redeemed ones: "After the suffering of his soul, he will see the light of life" (Isaiah 53:11).

Jesus was born to die…so that I could be born again to new life. It is the miracle of a violent grace: God securing for us the priceless treasures of His grace—one violence at a time.

Will you open your heart to receive now these costly gifts from your loving Savior?

PRAYER

Lord Jesus, You knew from the beginning
what the cost would be, and yet still You came.
You took on flesh and blood
so that You could bleed and die, all for me.
Open the eyes of my heart, Lord.
Let me see what it means that You were born
only so that You could die
and that You died only to make it possible
for me to be born again.
And as You enable me to see, Lord,
let me live in like measure
by Your grace.

Amen

ISAIAH 53:1–12

Who has believed our message and to whom
has the arm of the LORD been revealed?

He grew up before him like a tender shoot,
and like a root out of dry ground.
He had no beauty or majesty to attract us to him,
nothing in his appearance that we should desire him.

He was despised and rejected by men,
a man of sorrows, and familiar with suffering.
Like one from whom men hide their faces
he was despised, and we esteemed him not.

Surely he took up our infirmities
and carried our sorrows,
yet we considered him stricken by God,
smitten by him, and afflicted.

But he was pierced for our transgressions,
he was crushed for our iniquities;
the punishment that brought us peace was upon him,
and by his wounds we are healed.

We all, like sheep, have gone astray,
each of us has turned to his own way;
and the LORD has laid on him
the iniquity of us all.

He was oppressed and afflicted,
yet he did not open his mouth;
he was led like a lamb to the slaughter,
and as a sheep before her shearers is silent,
so he did not open his mouth.

By oppression and judgment he was taken away.
And who can speak of his descendants?
For he was cut off from the land of the living;
for the transgression of my people he was stricken.

He was assigned a grave with the wicked,
and with the rich in his death,
though he had done no violence,
nor was any deceit in his mouth.

Yet it was the LORD's will to crush him and
cause him to suffer, and though the LORD makes
his life a guilt offering,
he will see his offspring and prolong his days,
and the will of the LORD will prosper in his hand.

After the suffering of his soul,
he will see the light of
life and be satisfied;
by his knowledge my righteous
servant will justify many,
and he will bear their iniquities.

Therefore I will give him a portion among the great,
and he will divide the spoils with the strong,
because he poured out his life unto death,
and was numbered with the transgressors.
For he bore the sin of many,
and made intercession for the transgressors.

HE SUFFERED TEMPTATION
SO I CAN EXPERIENCE VICTORY

*My soul is overwhelmed
with sorrow to the point of death.*

MATTHEW 26:38

The most amazing three years of ministry ever recorded started with a full-scale assault in the desert.

The target was Jesus.

The adversary? Satan himself.

On that occasion, Jesus refused to surrender, choosing instead to hold on to the Father's destiny for His life. No pleasure, no power, no personal gain could deter Him from His world-saving mission.

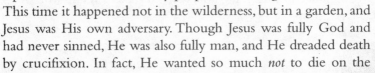

Jesus' ministry closed with another assault— a personal attack on His very purpose for living. This time it happened not in the wilderness, but in a garden, and Jesus was His own adversary. Though Jesus was fully God and had never sinned, He was also fully man, and He dreaded death by crucifixion. In fact, He wanted so much *not* to die on the cross that He confessed to His disciples, "My soul is over-whelmed with sorrow to the point of death" (Matthew 26:38).

The *overwhelmed* soul of Jesus….

Have you ever felt that you'd rather die than keep going?

Gethsemane, the garden where Jesus' awful drama played itself out, means *place of crushing.* The name came from the olive press located there. You can imagine how an olive press works: Beautiful, ripe olives go in; heavy stones apply irresistible pressure; and the precious oil flows out. All that remains in the press is unrecognizable pulp.

For just such a crushing, Jesus has come to Gethsemane. Before the night is over, there will be a series of struggles, and in each one, He will be crushed. Two days later, the human form of the Son of God will have been beaten and battered beyond recognition. But from His crushing, precious and abundant life will flow for you and me. Without the sorrows of Gethsemane, there will be no salvation at Golgotha.

After more than thirty years of vibrant life, it is here that Jesus starts to die. This quiet garden is the beginning of the end for Him.

Three times during these hours, Jesus entreats the Father to spare Him from death on the cross. Mark tells us that Jesus used the language of a child: "Abba [Daddy!]," He cried, "Father, everything is possible for you. Take this cup from me." (Mark 14:36).

Most of us wouldn't normally associate temptation with violence. But the word the Gospels use for sorrow is *agonia,* from which we derive the word "agony." It is based on the noun *agon,* which originally referred to a place where athletic contests were held or an arena where gladiators fought to certain death. These words capture Jesus' violent struggle as He prayed: He was wrestling, striving against great odds, *agonizing* with every breath.

Luke's account of the Garden of Gethsemane gives two unique details. First, he tells us that an angel appeared to strengthen Jesus (Luke 22:43). Since the disciples couldn't stay awake to help, God sent one of His ministering spirits to comfort His Son. But Jesus was beyond comfort, even the comfort of an angel. Luke adds:

> *And being in anguish, he prayed more earnestly, and his sweat was like drops of blood falling to the ground. (22:44)*

Scholars love to argue about what Luke meant. Some say that he was merely using a figure of speech and that it was his way of showing that Jesus was sweating profusely. Others read the passage literally. They refer to a medical condition known as *hematidrosis,* whereby, under extreme stress, the capillaries dilate to the point that they burst, releasing blood through the sweat glands. Luke was a physician, and, given his attention to medical details, I tend to prefer the second, literal interpretation. In the physical crush of anguish, Jesus literally sweated blood.

After more than thirty years of vibrant life, it is here that Jesus starts to die. This quiet garden is the beginning of the end.

However you interpret this passage, I hope you don't miss the central point: Jesus was fighting for His life. And it was a real fight, not just a theological one. "He himself suffered when he was tempted," insists the author of Hebrews, and "has been tempted in every way, just as we are" (Hebrews 2:18; 4:15).

In Gethsemane, Jesus is locked in combat with a human desire we all recognize: to avoid pain, to hold onto life, to win against death. In these dark night hours, while His best friends nod off, Jesus' flesh and feelings are at war. "If it's possible…," He groans.

Do you see what is at stake for us in that struggle? If Jesus' human desire does not lose, we will *never* win. If he doesn't suffer this temptation, we will *never* be able to overcome when we are tempted.

Until Gethsemane, Jesus' life has been one continual yes to the Father. And that doesn't change this night in the garden. The only begotten Son is on a mission of love—a mission that He affirmed in that first assault in the desert—and the Father's desire is for Jesus to finish the work He has been sent to do.

Where does Jesus find the strength to overcome? I find the answer in seven perfect words:

Not my will, but thine be done.

When you think about it, every temptation we face gets its power from our desire to say yes to ourselves—to our own rights, wants, and needs—and no to God. The Bible's word for that response is disobedience. It's a pattern that began with Adam and Eve. Surely the serpent deceived them when he tempted them to taste the forbidden fruit, just as Satan often deceives us in our moments of testing. But deception is just the bait. The trap is always sprung by a clear choice to disobey God—to say, "Not thy will, but mine be done."

At Gethsemane, although Satan has done his best to confuse and deceive Him, Jesus chooses painful obedience. If choice is one side of the coin in overcoming temptation, then cost is the other. To make a choice is to slay the alternative. "Life is in the blood," declares the law (Leviticus 17:11, 14; Deuteronomy 12:23), and every dark drop that trickles down Jesus' cheek is proof of what the Savior is willing to pay for you and me.

Do you see what is at stake for us in that struggle? If Jesus' human desire does not lose, we will never win.

Not my will, but thine be done.

He is willing to lose all so that we can win all.

∽◌∾

"In your struggle against sin, you have not yet resisted to the point of shedding your blood," the writer of Hebrews told a group of believers who were about to enter their own dark Gethsemane experience (Hebrews 12:4).

We must make the choice to say yes or no to the Father every day. Many will face severe testing on some critical issue of obedience in the days to come. Will I be asked to shed my blood for my faith? Probably not. But today believers around the world are honoring Christ in exactly that way.

Thankfully for us, whatever the test, Jesus won a break-through victory over temptation in Gethsemane: "Because he himself suffered when he was tempted, he is able to help those who are being tempted" (Hebrews 2:18). Unlike Jesus' solitary struggle, we are never alone when our times of crushing come. He has gone before us; He has faced the worst that life has to offer. And, though it might seem otherwise, He remains by our side every minute.

The help Jesus gives us now is both the *will* to make the choice to obey and the *grace* to pay the cost—no matter how bloody. By His Spirit's power, we, too, can respond, "Not my will, but thine be done." Jesus' agonizing battle with temptation—while His best friends slept and His flesh melted with pain—secured for us forever the power to overcome it.

Through the shadows of the garden the soldiers approach, armed to the teeth. The assault in Gethsemane is over. The initial engagement has been won. Now the final war is about to begin.

PRAYER

Jesus, I have not resisted temptation
to the point of shedding blood, as You did.
But even now the darkness of personal assault
is pressing in on me and many others whom You love.
Thank You for Your victory in the garden.
How I praise You for speaking those seven
perfect words for me and to me.
I take them as my victory cry today:
Not my will, but thine be done.
You have given me the words,
the will, and the grace I need to obey You completely.
All I ask now, Lord,
is that You would remain with me in every test I face.
And I worship You because You will.

Amen

HE WAS BETRAYED
SO I MIGHT KNOW HIS FAITHFULNESS

Rise, let us go!
Here comes my betrayer!

MATTHEW 26:46

he disciples called Him Lord, Master, Rabbi, the
Christ. Jesus called them simply "friends." He urged them to
"love each other as I have loved you" (John 15:12).

But that night in Gethsemane, the disciples' love for Jesus
was not apparent. They dozed off rather than keep Him company during His agonizing vigil. Peter was soon to prove
disloyal. And the one disciple who hadn't been
present in the garden earlier turned from friend
to betrayer—and sealed his betrayal with a kiss.

3

Judas knew Jesus would be in the garden. John tells us that the
disciples gathered there often (John 18:2). As Jesus returns to the

cluster of sleeping disciples for the final time, the clatter of armor suddenly breaks the silence. Soldiers and temple guards march up, holding torches aloft and wielding swords and clubs. Then, as the startled disciples watch, Judas steps forward.

"Greetings, Rabbi," he says, and leans to kiss Jesus.

"Friend," Jesus replies, "do what you came for" (Matthew 26:47–50).

In the Israel of that time, a kiss of greeting was a sign of honor and trust, but in the centuries since, a Judas kiss has come to stand for the worst kind of deception. I wonder: *Compared to the whips, thorns, and nails that were to come, was the kiss of a friend the worst violence of all?*

∽

A fairly good case can be made that until the betrayal, Judas was one of Jesus' closest friends. Jesus had chosen him to be one of the Twelve and entrusted him with the money bag—not a responsibility Jesus would have given lightly. A reconstruction of the seating arrangement at the Last Supper indicates that, while John was sitting at Jesus' right hand, the place of the honored guest, Judas was sitting at Jesus' left, which in the ancient world was known as "the place of the intimate friend."

I'm reminded of the psalm that says, "Even my close friend, whom I trusted, he who shared my bread, has lifted up his heel against me" (Psalm 41:9).

Still, Jesus had known from the beginning what Judas would do (John 6:64). What, then, was their relationship like? Jesus instructed His disciples to take life one day at a time. Is that what He did with Judas? The Gospels tell us that the disciples, having been sent out on their first mission, "returned with joy" (Luke

10:17). Didn't Judas have success stories to tell of his own ministry? Wouldn't he have celebrated Christ's new kingdom with the rest of the disciples? It doesn't seem likely that he simply lurked on the sidelines all those months.

But something went terribly wrong. Judas turned against his friend. Though people love to speculate about Judas's motive, the Gospels make it clear. He asked the high priest, "What are you willing to give me if I hand him over to you?" (Matthew 26:15). Judas betrayed Jesus for money.

For both betrayer and betrayed, Judas's treachery ended in violence. As his scheme fell apart, his world began to crumble. According to Matthew, when Judas realized that Jesus was going to die, he was seized with remorse. In a panic of guilt and regret, he tried to return the blood money. "I have sinned," Judas moaned, "for I have betrayed innocent blood." But the priests refused to take back the thirty pieces of silver. From trusted disciple and intimate friend, Judas had sunk first to traitor, then to murderer. His guilt was more than he could bear, and he went out and hanged himself (Matthew 27:3–5).

It's hard to understand how Judas, after so many months in the company of Christ, could have missed the big picture: all those sad, sick people touched with mercy and healing; all those demonstrations of the power of repentance. But apparently Judas's heart remained untouched and unchanged. If he could not bear to live with his sin, neither, it seems, could he imagine living for the Lord.

I take Judas's story as a warning to all who refuse the gift of grace that Jesus offers. Such refusal leads ultimately to confusion, betrayal, and death.

Peter's story is different. Certainly, he failed as a friend, too. To me, his betrayal of Jesus, though less deceitful, is more heartrending. In Judas, we don't see much passion for Jesus. Mostly we sense caution and criticism. But Peter soared from the start. He always led with his heart. He was the first to recognize the Christ; first to step into the waves in faith; first to declare, "Lord, I am ready to go with you to prison and to death" (Luke 22:33). When the soldiers came to arrest Jesus, it was Peter who drew his sword and attacked (John 18:10).

And then fear and doubt set in.

∽⦿

As Jesus is led away in chains, the disciples desert Him. Following at a safe distance, Peter ends up huddled beside a fire in the court-yard of the chief priest, where Jesus has been taken. Only a few yards separate Lord and disciple. But, blending into the crowd, Peter pretends not to know Him. Then a servant girl recognizes him. When she looks him in the eye and says, "You also were with Jesus of Galilee," Peter denies it. When the girl insists that he is one of Jesus' followers, Peter again denies it. But his Galilean accent gives him away, and others around him begin to repeat the girl's accusation. For the third time, in a barrage of curses, Peter denies his Lord. (Matthew 26:69–75).

Jesus, bound in chains across the courtyard, turns and looks straight at Peter. His gentle look breaks His disciple's heart, and Peter flees the scene, weeping bitterly (Luke 22:61).

Thankfully, Peter's story doesn't end in suicide. He is one of those who rush to the tomb on Easter morning (Luke 24:12), and he is present in the upper room when Jesus appears to Thomas (John 20:26).

But faithful Lord and fickle friend are on course for a per-sonal encounter. It happens when Peter and six of the other ten disciples return to their fishing nets. This incident is often called the second miraculous catch of fish, but in reality, it is Peter who is caught for the second time.

While the men are in the boat, Jesus appears on the shore.

"Friends," He calls. "You haven't caught anything, have you?"

"No, not one!" they shout back, not recognizing the stranger on the beach.

"Throw your nets on the other side and you'll find some," He calls. As soon as they do, their net is filled with fish.

John is the first to recognize Jesus, but Peter is the first to act. Impetuous as always, he immediately jumps into the water and starts swimming to shore.

In the conversation that follows, Jesus asks Peter three times, "Do you love me?" Three times Peter answers, "Yes, Lord, You know I love You." Jesus' repetition unnerves Peter. He doesn't realize that Jesus is offering him exactly as many chances to affirm his love as the number of times Peter has denied it.

There must be more to say because Jesus invites Peter to walk with Him. And Peter does—for the rest of his life.

Even my close friend, whom I trusted, he who shared my bread, has lifted up his heel against me.

PSALM 41:9

❦

Skip ahead several decades.

In two letters to believers, a mature Peter shines forth. Still fiery, yes. Still sure. But the gospel has gentled him. As an elderly leader of the infant church, Peter's impetuosity is gone, but his passion has deepened.

Why the transformation? I think we can trace it to that reckless leap into the sea of grace. Unlike Judas, Peter reached out again for the gifts of friendship that Jesus offered—forgiveness, acceptance, and a new start.

Maybe while Peter was fishing that day, he had been thinking about something Jesus had said: "Greater love has no one than this, that he lay down his life for his friends. You are my friends…" (John 15:13–14). Maybe he was hoping for another chance when Jesus appeared.

Now listen to Peter's testimony late in life:

> *Praise be to the God and Father of our Lord Jesus Christ! In his great mercy he has given us new birth into a living hope through the resurrection of Jesus Christ from the dead…. Though you have not seen him, you love him; and even though you do not see him now, you believe in him and are filled with an inexpressible and glorious joy, for you are receiving the goal of your faith, the salvation of your souls.*

(1 PETER 1:3, 8–9)

Both scenes were dark with shadows the night Jesus was betrayed. Some shadows fell among the groves of Gethsemane; others around the flickering of a makeshift fire. But the deeper darkness lay in the hearts of two men, Judas and Peter.

Judas refused forgiveness and turned first to despair and then to death. Peter chose grace and life. Peter's life is proof that because of Jesus' undying loyalty to us, we have the power today to become His faithful friends, disciples, servants, and joyful ministers of His limitless grace.

PRAYER

Lord Jesus—You who were betrayed and
who go on being betrayed—
grant me the courage to stand faithfully for You
in every situation, no matter the cost.
Transform my fearfulness and fickleness into faithfulness.
When Your eye searches me today,
may You find me loyal and true.
May You never see betrayal in my actions
or hear denial from my lips.
How much I long to be your faithful friend, O Lord!
Thank You for Your steadfast love.
You are my friend to the end of time.

Amen

HE WAS ARRESTED AND BOUND
SO I COULD BE RESCUED FROM BONDAGE

*The men seized Jesus
and arrested him.*

MARK 14:46

*I*t takes some work for us to reclaim for our imaginations the true picture of the arrest of Jesus. Some of you might see in your mind's eye the richly painted, perfectly posed scene often depicted in classical art. Others of us are stuck with a cardboard and plastic version we've seen acted out in some church basement. In fact, the confrontation unfolded more like a torch-lit nightmare. A worn and bleeding Christ. A treacherous kiss. Shaken disciples. Confusion. Mutilation. Arrest. Panic. Flight.

It was no small, meandering band of soldiers who came to arrest Jesus, but a detachment of Roman legionnaires, almost certainly numbering more than two hundred. John uses the Greek technical term *speria,* which indicated one tenth of a legion, or six hundred men (John 18:3).

Accompanying them were Jewish religious officials and the temple guards. The Gospels tell us that they were armed with clubs and swords. The fact that they carried weapons indicates that they were expecting a confrontation with Jesus' followers, perhaps even a full-scale riot. Even though there would have been moonlight—Passover always fell on a full moon—the soldiers carried lanterns because they expected to have to comb the hillside for rebels in hiding.

Look into the soldiers' faces. What do you see? I see tension, discipline, brutality, prejudice, perhaps hatred.

What, I wonder, did Jesus see in those faces? In the faces of the priests, Pharisees, and temple guards Jesus saw fellow Jews who, in the name of His Father, wanted Him dead. He saw a friend who had turned against Him. He saw strangers who would mock and humiliate Him. He saw mercenaries who wouldn't flinch at pounding spikes into His flesh. He saw a centurion who would later look up at His lifeless body and, ironically, confess Him innocent (Mark 15:39).

This is just the kind of nighttime police action the Romans dread—a tough-to-control confrontation between rival religious factions. After all, it's their job to preserve the *Pax Romana,* the "peace of Rome." The last thing anyone expected is exactly what happens next: Jesus walks directly up to the mob.

"Who are you looking for?" He asks.

"Jesus of Nazareth," they reply.

"I am he," says Jesus.

Now pandemonium breaks out (John 18:6). The Romans, who take Jesus' declaration as a signal to hidden supporters, bark out commands and fall into a defensive military formation. The Jews drop to the ground—they have just heard a manifestation of the divine name, *I AM* (Exodus 3:14).

If ever there is a perfect chance to escape, now is the time.

But Jesus stays where He is, the serene center of a chaotic scene. Again He asks, "Who is it you are looking for?"

Three times Jesus tells His would-be captors, "I am he." Then, pointing to his frightened disciples, He says, "If you are looking for me, then let these men go."

At this moment Peter lunges at the nearest temple servant and cuts off his ear. I can imagine the Roman legionnaires jumping forward, ready to attack. But Jesus intervenes. "Put your sword away," He tells Peter and steps over to touch and heal the injured servant.

Finally, He turns to the Jews and asks, "Am I leading a rebellion, that you have come with swords and clubs? Every day I was with you in the temple courts, and you did not lay a hand on me" (Luke 22:52–53). With one direct question He points out their deceit and cowardice; with one pointed remark He informs them that they have the power to arrest Him now only because the Father wills it. For years Jesus has acted and spoken openly in public. To treat Him like a common thief now is a shameful act.

Nevertheless, the soldiers seize Him and bind His hands. Jesus does not resist. The one who measured the oceans in the hollow of His hands (Isaiah 40:12) chooses to be powerless. As

The soldiers seize Him and bind His hands. Jesus does not resist. The one who measured the oceans in the hollow of His hands chooses to be powerless.

the disciples flee, the soldiers lead Jesus away under guard. The one who has twelve legions of angels at His command (Matthew 26:53) chooses to go with them.

"Where are you taking Him?" someone asks.

"To the authorities," the soldiers reply, "to make sure He gets the punishment He deserves."

"Into captivity," Jesus would say, "to make certain you will be set free."

Throughout His ordeal, Jesus will refuse to cling to His power, just as He will refuse to protest His innocence. Instead, He will embrace weakness in order to expose the impotence of worldly justice. His debility will become our greatest strength. His guilt will purchase our innocence.

Once when Jesus promised them freedom, the Jews were offended. "We've never been slaves of anyone!" they exclaimed. "How can you say that we shall be set free?"

"If the Son sets you free, you will be free indeed," Jesus replied (John 8:33, 36).

They thought He was talking about being set free from the Romans. But He was talking about freedom from sin and self and every kind of human bondage—the kind of slavery that so enchains our being that the price of freedom had to be this: Jesus tied up like a common thief and led away under arrest.

❧

Everyone is gone now. Gethsemane is quiet, wrapped in shadows again. A discarded torch sputters out in the dust. The moon reigns in silence above the olive trees.

When I think about the night that Jesus was arrested, it floats in my imagination like a photographic negative—the dark is light, the light is dark—and the bondage of Jesus is freedom for me.

And I am free indeed.

PRAYER

Master, the highest blessings, praise,

and thanks to You for my freedom!

I was a captive to my own sin,

and I hardly knew it,

but You set me free with Your word of truth.

Step in to save me, Lord,

whenever I try to return to that awful bondage.

Make my heart glad as I submit to Your easy yoke,

so that I may exult in the freedom

of serving You forever.

Amen

HE STOOD TRIAL ALONE
SO I MIGHT HAVE AN ADVOCATE

*Then the whole assembly rose
and led him off to Pilate.*

LUKE 23:1

After His arrest, Jesus is led in to face a hastily convened council of Jewish leaders. Caiaphas, chief priest of the Sanhedrin, presides over the kangaroo court (John 18:24).

His religious enemies wait to hear just one thing—Jesus' claiming to be the Messiah and the Son of God. That claim is a heresy that Jewish law says is punishable by death. When Jesus makes the claim, they have what they need. "Why do we need any more testimony?" they ask. "We have heard it from his own lips" (Luke 22:71).

The next stop is the Roman governor, Pontius Pilate. Since the Jews will not enter the palace for fear of becoming ceremonially unclean, Pilate begrudgingly comes out to them, and they present their case against Jesus on the palace steps. A vague charge of religious trespass doesn't carry much weight with the Roman governor, so the Jewish leaders recast their brief.

"We have found this man subverting our nation," they tell Pilate. "He opposes payment of taxes to Caesar and claims to be Christ, a king" (Luke 23:2).

At every step of the proceedings Jesus' enemies were there to press their case. But where was the counsel for the defense?

Thinks he shouldn't pay taxes? Thinks he's a king? You can imagine Pilate pondering the charges brought with such urgency so early in the morning. *This rebellious province is full of people like that!* With barely a flicker of interest, he tells the religious leaders that they don't have a case.

Relieved to learn that Jesus is from Galilee, Pilate then tells them to take the case to King Herod, who has jurisdiction for Galilee and who is in Jerusalem for Passover. The entourage troops off to Herod's palace.

Herod is happy to see Jesus, but not for any legal, political, or theological reason. "He hoped to see him perform some miracle," writes Luke (Luke 23:8). Although Herod asks Him many questions, Jesus refuses to answer him. So Herod and his soldiers ridicule and mock him, dress him up as a make-believe king, and send him back to Pilate. Whether he wants to or not, Pilate will decide Christ's fate.

∽

You've noticed, I'm sure, that at every step of the proceedings Jesus' enemies were there to press their case. But where was the counsel for the defense? Nowhere to be found. In Jesus' day the sole responsibility for the fairness of a trial fell to the magistrate—in this case, Pontius Pilate.

Yet, since we read in every Gospel account that Pilate found no fault in Jesus and wanted to set Him free, we have to ask: What happened to justice? Why did Pilate change his mind? Matthew even says that Pilate's wife, Claudia Porcula, had dreamed about Jesus and sent word to her husband: "Don't have anything to do with that innocent man" (Matthew 27:19).

To help you understand why Pilate's name ended up going down in history as synonymous for cowardice and injustice, come with me behind the scenes.

∽◯◯

The Palestine of Jesus' day was a region in transition. Between 30 B.C. and A.D. 14, during the reign of Octavian, the Roman Republic was transformed into an empire. In the new order, leaders in various parts of the Empire often had to scramble to hold on to their power.

Pilate was no exception. He had received the governorship because of the patronage of a powerful senator in Rome, Lucius Aelius Sejanus, who held the favored position as consul to the Emperor Tiberius, Octavian's successor. Sejanus was well known for his hatred of the troublesome Jews. In fact, in A.D. 19 Sejanus persuaded Tiberius to expel all Jews from Rome.

Like his patron, Pilate displayed an open disdain for the people of Palestine. To build an aqueduct for Jerusalem, he stole money from the temple treasury, which caused a riot in Jerusalem. Soldiers disguised in plain clothes infiltrated the crowd and slaughtered hundreds of people.

In another incident, he set up the soldiers' standards outside the temple. These symbolic poles usually depicted the bust of the emperor, and the soldiers burned incense to them during military campaigns. The Jews therefore considered them graven images.

Putting them near the temple led to a Roman confrontation with a Jewish mob in the amphitheater in Caesarea. On this occasion, Pilate backed down and ordered the standards removed.

Pilate also issued coins for the region that were stamped with the *littus* and the *simpulum*—the stick and the ladle used in pagan offerings. There is no record of the response of Jewish leaders, but it's not hard to imagine.

Finally, just before Pilate appeared on the steps of his palace for Jesus' trial, something happened that put his political future on the line. In A.D. 31, Pilate's patron, Sejanus, had been exposed as a liar. The accusations that had led to the Jewish expulsion turned out to have no basis in fact. On October 18, Tiberius had him executed. Then he ordered hostilities against the Jews to cease and dismissed many of Sejanus's appointees. Pilate must have wondered if he would be next.

At the time of Jesus' trial, Pilate's grasp on power depended entirely on proving that he had transferred his loyalty from his former patron to Tiberius. His actions during the trial revealed that he was determined to stay in power.

Pilate, the anti-Semite, clearly enjoyed goading the priests and Pharisees, and he relished this opportunity to embarrass the Jewish leaders. When they protested the wording of the inscription he placed above Jesus' cross, Pilate coolly responded, "What I have written, I have written" (John 19:22).

Pilate, the judge, recognized the jealousy behind the spurious charges the Jews had brought against Jesus. As the administrator of Roman justice, he found Jesus not guilty, for "he knew it was out of envy that they had handed Jesus over to him" (Matthew 27:18).

And what about Pilate, the politician? With sinking hearts, we see that his insight into the motives of Jesus' enemies and his finding that Jesus was innocent were not enough to determine his course. His ultimate concern had nothing to do with governing justly and everything to do with using his position to stay in power.

Pilate's ultimate concern had nothing to do with governing justly and everything to do with staying in power.

⊱⊰

Does this last statement make you wonder about Pilate's most famous question during the trial proceedings?

We read about it in John 18. Jesus has just told Pilate that He has, indeed, been born to be king and that one purpose of kingship is to testify to the truth.

"Everyone on the side of truth listens to me," Jesus says.

"What is truth?" Pilate asks in reply (John 18:37–38).

Many essays and sermons have been written on those three words: *What is truth?* Was Pilate wistful? Sincerely seeking? Sardonic? Defensive? Or was it merely an off-handed remark?

The very next sentence begins: "With this [Pilate] went out again to the Jews…" (John 18:38). Pilate didn't even wait for an answer. He immediately turned and walked away. His question was meaningless—the empty rhetoric of politics—and he was already sure of the answer: Truth was what served his political purposes at the time.

John's Gospel records the turning point in the proceedings against Jesus. Pilate has decided that Jesus should go free. Then someone in the crowd shouts, "If you let this man go, you are no friend of Caesar" (John 19:12). "Friend of Caesar" was one of the formal titles for a Roman governor. Whoever shouted this knew that Pilate was standing on a slippery political slope. When Pilate heard it, he abandoned his defense of Jesus.

The stage was set for an unthinkable act: The official who was charged with upholding the truth handed over a man he knew was innocent to a murderous mob.

And Jesus went willingly.

The one who had no legal counsel and stood alone before His enemies stands today in the Father's presence as our eternal Advocate. "We have one who speaks to the Father in our defense—Jesus Christ, the Righteous One,"

1 John 2:1

He was oppressed and afflicted,
yet he did not open not his mouth....
By oppression and judgment, he was taken away....
For he was cut off from the land of the living;
For the transgression of my people he was stricken.

(Isaiah 53: 7–8)

What became of this man who tried Jesus and chose to send Him to His death?

Pilate was removed from office in A.D. 37 for excessive cruelty to the Jews. It is thought that he committed suicide on his final journey to Rome. According to tradition, his wife became a believer; she later came to be revered as a saint in the Greek Orthodox Church.

And what about the man condemned that day?

The one who had no legal counsel and stood alone before His

enemies stands today in the Father's presence as our eternal Advocate. "We have one who speaks to the Father in our defense—Jesus Christ, the Righteous One," wrote John many years after Jesus' trial (1 John 2:1).

Not only that, but Jesus, as He promised, has sent the Holy Spirit to be our counselor and comforter here on earth. *Parakletos,* the word Jesus used to describe the Spirit, means "to be called alongside." The Spirit is called alongside us, exactly like legal counsel in a court case. "The Spirit himself intercedes for us," Paul wrote (Romans 8:26).

Although Jesus stood alone to face His accusers, we never have to. When the powers of this world, seen and unseen, condemn us, Jesus is always standing alongside—not to protest our innocence, but to offer Himself as the one who has already stood trial for our sins.

PRAYER

Lord Jesus, on the day You were accused of wrongdoing,
neither You nor anyone else stood up for Your innocence.
You let Your condemnation stand, knowing that by doing so
You would provide for my release.
Now You Yourself are my Advocate
in the courts of heaven.
Thank You, loving Savior.
Transform my life by the knowledge
that no one can find me guilty;
I'm covered by Your righteousness.
Thank You for the gift of the Holy Spirit,
my counsel and comforter.
Help me listen to the Spirit's urgings today
and live always as a free man for Your sake.

Amen

HE WAS WOUNDED
SO I COULD BE HEALED

Then Pilate took
Jesus and had him flogged.

JOHN 19:1

*E*ight words. One sentence. A footnote before Calvary. But I can barely bring myself to write about this scene or ask you to think with me about what really happened.

Then Pilate took Jesus and had Him flogged.

Matthew and Mark tell the story just as briefly, then add, "and handed him over to be crucified" (Matthew 27:26; Mark 15:15).

This torture by beating had been on Jesus' mind for some time. He had warned His disciples early in His ministry that they might have to submit to being flogged. Almost every time He predicted His death, He referred to flogging (Mark 10:34; Luke 18:32). It appears in Old Testament prophecies as well:

> *My back is filled with searing pain. (Psalm 38:7)*
> *I offered my back to those who beat me. (Isaiah 50:6)*

The flogging of Jesus is the one aspect of His suffering that movies and preachers most consistently misrepresent. The popular image includes the counting of the stripes, usually accompanied by a lot of theatrics. This misunderstanding is based upon Paul's description of his flogging in the synagogue. "Five times I received from the Jews the forty lashes minus one," he wrote (2 Corinthians 11:24). His punishment was based on an Old Testament Deuteronomic law:

> *If the guilty man deserves to be beaten, the judge shall make him lie down and have him flogged in his presence with the number of lashes his crime deserves, but he must not give him more than forty lashes. If he is flogged more than that, your brother will be degraded in your eyes.*
>
> (DEUTERONOMY 25:2–3)

Romans, not Jews, flogged Jesus. The only stipulation Roman law made was that a man would be flogged until the flesh hung from his back.

But Romans, not Jews, flogged Jesus. While the Jews administered synagogue discipline with rods, Romans used what we would call a cat-o'-nine-tails. This instrument of torture consisted of long leather straps embedded with pieces of bone or glass. Occasionally lead balls were woven into the thongs to increase the impact of the blows. And while the law of Moses stipulated a maximum of forty lashes minus one, no such limit existed in Roman law or practice.

Josephus revealed the ferocity of Roman flogging when, commenting on the fate of a prisoner of the Jewish War, he said that the man was lacerated to the bone with scourges. In fact, the only stipulation Roman law made was that a man would be flogged until the flesh hung from his back. The blows fell until the skin split open and the muscles were severed; until ligaments tore and bone chipped. Some men were disemboweled. Many did not survive.

To intensify the suffering of the victim, flogging *always* preceded a crucifixion. As an unintentional mercy, it could hasten death when it resulted in a massive loss of blood.

Some scholars think that Jesus may have been flogged twice.

Some scholars think that Jesus may have been flogged twice. The accounts of both Luke and John hint at it. Medical doctors who have studied the accounts of the crucifixion have concluded that severe multiple beatings would account for the fact that Jesus died after only six hours on the cross, while others were known to have hung on crosses for as long as nine days before dying from exhaustion and loss of blood.

∽◯◯

Imagine it with me.

Jesus is standing there stripped, shackled, and alone in the circle. The legionnaire steps forward, opens his reach, and begins. The scourges hiss through the air in a wide arc and sink with a thud in Christ's skin.

The crowd howls.

The scourges rise again and again in the soldier's fist. And fall. And rise again.

Soldiers sneer and spit. The scourges hiss and thud into purple flesh. Blood flows. God's chosen people scream for more.

The tormentor grunts and sweats, but keeps reaching back for that terrible, wide arc.

Jesus crumples. Guards rush to jerk Him to His feet. The scourges rise again, and fall.

Look! The righteous anger of God, diverted for all time, is pouring down on this man, His Son.

But the fault is mine, and I must look away.

∽◯∾

It is one thing to speak in theological terms about an obligatory sacrifice for a fallen world. It is an entirely different thing to stand in the presence of brutal men and their instruments of torture and try to watch, realizing that Jesus endured all that and more for you and me.

Yet His pain was the prelude to the outpouring of God's favor. By enduring the violence in that circle of hate, Jesus accomplished a costly exchange. With each blow, He carried away our grief and our brokenness and bought back for us—for that howling mob and for every person since—the treasures of grace.

"By his wounds we are healed," wrote Isaiah. Healing through wounding; wholeness through brokenness. That is the way of the cross—the way of Jesus. It is the method of an upside-down kingdom, whose king dies for his subjects.

> Surely he took up our infirmities
> and carried our sorrows,
> yet we considered him stricken by God,
> smitten by him, and afflicted.
> He was crushed for our iniquities;
> the punishment that brought us peace was upon him,
> and by his wounds we are healed.

(ISAIAH 53:4–5)

PRAYER

Jesus, I worship You today in awe and humility.

Thank You, suffering Redeemer,

for paying the price for me.

Pour out on me the healing power

that flows from Your woundedness.

Make well the sickness of my soul

by the sickness unto death that You suffered.

And through me in some small or large way today,

bring Your priceless redemption to others.

Amen

HE ENDURED MOCKERY
SO I COULD KNOW DIGNITY AND JOY

The men...began mocking...him.

LUKE 22:63

Can you remember a humiliation from childhood that seemed to burn a hole in your heart? You wore the wrong clothes and kids teased you. You said the wrong thing at the wrong time at the top of your voice. Your clumsiness in gym class made you the butt of the teacher's jokes.

Though I do not possess an especially good memory, at any given moment I can recall with perfect clarity an incident that happened to me more than thirty-five years ago. In the scene, I am in the junior high lunchroom with my head buried in my hands, weeping bitterly. Surrounding me are perhaps fifteen children my age, some of them my good friends. They are pointing and laughing at me because someone has spilled milk on my clothes.

It was not my fault. I was innocent. At the instant it happened, I looked around to see how those who saw it would respond, expecting them either to laugh with me or ridicule the person who spilled the milk. But at the instigation of one boy, they all turned on me. It sounds like a foolish thing, but to this day, if I think about it long enough, I still get angry to tears over it. I was mocked, though I was innocent.

The particulars of the incident are not what matter. It is the feeling of shame and outrage at the injustice—the verbal violence of the thing—that cuts us so deeply.

Why would one person mock another? I think it's because we want to be on the winning side. If a group can isolate someone and push him down, everyone who participates feels stronger. They are reassured that they are right and—unlike the poor fool who is the target—well liked by the rest.

> *The men...
> began mocking
> and beating
> him. They
> blindfolded him
> and demanded,
> "Prophesy!
> Who hit you?"
> And they said
> many other
> insulting things
> to him.*
>
> LUKE 22:63

On the day of Jesus' journey to Calvary, a lot of people decided He was a fool. A perfect target for mockery.

❧

It starts with the religious leaders.

Bound and blindfolded, Jesus has been dragged before Caiaphas, the high priest, and other religious leaders. There they put Him on trial as an imposter. "Are you the Son of God?" they demand contemptuously.

When Jesus replies, "It is as you say," Caiaphas tears his clothes in horror at such blasphemy. I can imagine the pious onlookers shouting and pointing fingers at the forlorn figure. "Son of God? Messiah? Him?"

Very quickly, Jesus' mockers turn from verbal to physical attacks. "They spit in his face and struck him with their fists," Matthew writes. Others slap Him. "Prophesy to us, Christ! Who hit you?" the temple guards taunt (Matthew 26:67–68). We can hear the poison dripping from every word.

The mockery continues throughout Jesus' ordeal that day:

> *His guards make fun of him. (Luke 22:63–65)*
> *Herod and his men ridicule him. (Luke 23:11)*
> *The Roman centurions who flogged him jeer at him. (Matthew 27:29)*

And on the long, stumbling walk up to Golgotha, Jesus' plight turns to sport for the masses. "I endure scorn for your sake," David had prophesied, "and shame covers my face" (Psalm 69:7). The good citizens of Jerusalem hurl curses at the condemned man as He staggers by. Mothers hold up their children to laugh at Him. Fathers and sons spit in His face.

Mockery is verbal violence. And Jesus is subjected to it all the way to the place of His execution.

Good citizens hurl curses at the condemned man as He staggers by. Mothers hold up their children to laugh at Him. Fathers and sons spit in His face.

We can divide the mockers at Golgotha into groups.

The soldiers assigned the task of executing Jesus
These men were almost certainly mercenaries—killers for hire—in the Roman army. Gentiles from various parts of the empire, they would have had only a nodding acquaintance with Jewish customs. For them, Jews were a mysterious and unpredictable lot, and a crucifixion was just another day's work.

Compared to other forms of execution, a crucifixion at least gave them the pleasure of tormenting their victims. They took delight in nailing the written charge against Christ on the *titulus* above His head: "King of the Jews."

"If you are King of the Jews," they shouted as Jesus writhed on the cross, "save yourself!" They defied Him to unfasten even one nail.

Their "if" reminds me of Satan's temptation of Jesus in the wilderness: "If you are the Son of God...." And again, even though Jesus was both King and Son, He refused to prove it. Instead, He humbled Himself and became, in Paul's words, "obedient to death—even death on a cross" (Philippians 2:8).

The priests, Pharisees, and lawyers who prosecuted Jesus
From the very beginning these religious leaders had incited the rabble against Jesus. They were the ones who proposed swapping Barabbas alive for Jesus dead. They were the first to cry, "Crucify him!" (Mark 15:13).

Even when their victory over Jesus seemed certain, they persisted in their mockery. But, unlike the Roman soldiers, these religious leaders taunted Jesus in theological ways. "He saved others," they shouted, "but he can't save himself!" And "Let him come down from the cross, and we will believe in him"

(Matthew 27:42). Salvation and belief—these were their categories, yet they didn't realize that Jesus had utterly redefined these ideas. They didn't understand that by not saving Himself, this bleeding man would save all mankind.

What they needed in order to change their minds, they shouted, was a sign. But—have you noticed?—people who demand signs rarely believe them when they do happen. After all, Jesus had already raised the dead. He had already fed thousands, cured the sick, and healed the lame. These religious leaders had all the evidence they needed if they were truly open to belief. But they were not.

The passersby who watched Jesus die

Roman law dictated that crucifixions occur only in the most public of places so that it would have the greatest possible impact on other potential rebels and criminals. And this was Passover, the one week of the year that Jerusalem was packed with Jews from far and wide. Taken together, these circumstances indicate that hundreds, perhaps thousands, witnessed Jesus' crucifixion. Matthew and Mark reported that these crowds of passersby were "shaking their heads and hurling insults at him" (Matthew 27:39; Mark 15:29).

I picture the people standing around in groups near the cross trading "Jesus stories." "See that wreck of a man up there?" they say to whoever will listen. "He claimed that if the temple were torn down, He could rebuild it in three days!"

They are right about Christ's claim. Once, after routing the vendors from the temple marketplace, Jesus had said, "Destroy this temple, and I will raise it again in three days" (John 2:19; Mark 14:58). But, as with nearly every other deeply spiritual statement He made, they misunderstood His meaning. He was referring not to Herod's building, but to His own body and its future resurrection. It was simply beyond their ability to understand.

The Jews' outrage over Jesus' claim stemmed from their vehement attachment to the temple *(ha makom),* "the place." The magnificent building, begun by Herod the Great, had been under construction for forty-six years and wouldn't be completed for thirty more. Yet in A.D. 70, only six years after its completion, the Romans would destroy the temple in their attack on Jerusalem, leaving (as Jesus had predicted) not one stone upon another.

Now, as Jesus hangs dying on the cross, onlookers reopen the old wound. "You who are going to destroy the temple and build it in three days... save yourself!" (Mark 15:29–30).

The charge would surface again less than two years later when it was brought against Stephen because of his relationship with the one who had spoken of destroying "this place" (Acts 6:14). Like his Master, Stephen would die.

The criminals who were crucified with Jesus
You might expect that the other victims that day would have treated Jesus with more understanding, but that wasn't the case. Both Matthew and Mark say that they "heaped insults on him" (Matthew 27:44; Mark 15:32). Luke even records the words of one of them: "Aren't you the Christ? Save yourself and us!" (Luke 23:39). Their rejection of Him puts the finishing touches on the portrait of an abandoned and vilified Savior and fulfills the prophecy of David: "All who see me mock me" (Psalm 22:7).

We could safely say that the last words Jesus heard in the moments before His death were insults.

If spit was on His face and scorn was in His ears, what do you think was in Jesus' heart? For a surprising clue to how Jesus responded, turn to a familiar verse in the book of Hebrews:

> *Let us fix our eyes on Jesus, the author and perfecter*
> *of our faith, who for the joy set before him endured*
> *the cross, scorning its shame.*

(HEBREWS 12:2)

Could the experts from the temple have ever conceived of a God who would endure the cross, scorning the shame of it, for *joy?* I don't think so. Could the soldiers and passersby that day have guessed it from the condition of Christ's body? Never. Did the criminals who hung on either side of Jesus sense it, even just a little? One of them, perhaps....

I wonder: What was it about the "joy set before Him" that literally allowed Jesus to scorn the mockery? It certainly didn't prevent Him from experiencing every nerve ending of pain and hours of humiliation. Yet He endured—for the joy. Jesus could rise above the mockery of the moment because He soared on the wings of eternal truth:

- As God's Son, He understood that He possessed a hidden and untouchable dignity.
- He knew beyond a doubt that He could look forward to the eternal glory that the Father was reserving for Him.
- And, as one whose whole heart was intent on bringing redemption to others, He was convinced that each violence was allowed

*only so that—through it and in spite of it—He could bring
salvation and healing to a hurting world.*

Amazingly, these same eternal truths describe every believer
in Christ today. As adopted sons and daughters of the King and
heirs of His kingdom, we possess a dignity of which the mocking world is unaware. We, too, look forward to enjoying God's
glory for eternity. And our purpose on this earth is also to be
agents of redemption in Christ's name.

When scorn and ridicule come, we never have to bury our
heads in our hands or lash out in hatred. Jesus has gone before.
Because He endured the scorn *for joy,* we can too.

PRAYER

My King, for the sake of the joy that was set before You,
You absorbed all the venomous cruelty
that others could pour out on You.
Enable me, Lord, to joyfully endure
the verbal and emotional violence
I might encounter today, especially any ridicule
that comes my way because I belong to You.
Give me the grace to fix my eyes on You,
who endured so much shame so that one day
I could be covered in Your glory.

Amen

HE WAS CONDEMNED
SO THE TRUTH COULD SET ME FREE

"If I spoke the truth,
why did you strike me?"

*Y*ou might have grown up reading all those "verily, verily"s in the King James Version of the Bible. Modern translations like the NIV translate that familiar phrase from Jesus' teachings as, "I tell you the truth." In the Gospels, Jesus uses the phrase eighty times.

More than the other Gospel writers, John emphasizes the theme that truth-telling was central to Jesus' mission on earth. He opens his account with this sweeping statement:

8

> *The Word became flesh and made his dwelling among us.*
> *We have seen his glory, the glory of the One and Only,*
> *who came from the Father, full of grace and truth.*

(JOHN 1:14)

Then John sets about to show that Jesus spoke the truth. A few examples:

- *Jesus to Nicodemus: "I tell you the truth, no one can see the kingdom of God unless he is born again." (3:3)*
- *Jesus teaching in the temple courts: "He who works for the honor of the one who sent him is a man of truth; there is nothing false about him." (7:18)*
- *Jesus to his new converts: "You will know the truth, and the truth will set you free." (8:32)*
- *Jesus to an angry mob: "You are determined to kill me, a man who has told you the truth that I heard from God." (8:40)*
- *Jesus to his anxious disciples: "I am the way and the truth and the life." (14:6)*
- *Jesus to Pilate during his own trial: "For this reason I was born, and for this I came into the world, to testify to the truth. Everyone on the side of truth listens to me." (18:37)*

And where does all that truth-telling get Jesus, we might ask? Not into the freedom He promised us, but into a world of trouble.

<hr/>

It's easy for us to say we love truth more than anything. We try to teach our children to speak it. We require it of our governments and our bank statements. We chisel the word into the granite of our courthouses. We swear to tell the whole of it and nothing but it before a judge.

But let's admit it: Truth can cause a lot of trouble when it collides with beliefs or behaviors that are wrong, but which we cherish. Then we must choose. Will we stand for the truth whatever the cost? Or will we deny it for the sake of convenience?

Some preachers have a great time bashing the people of Jesus' day for not having been more open to the truth that God was trying to reveal to them. But would you and I have responded any more admirably or courageously?

I'm not sure.

You see, Jesus' teachings turned the world upside-down for a lot of people—most of them good people. He shook them out of their comfortable ignorance. He would tell them things that were hard to understand and that they didn't want to hear. Or He would answer a question with another, more challenging question. Most difficult of all were the times He would simply present *Himself* as the answer.

John records that at one point in Jesus' ministry, Thomas asks him, "How can we know the way?" (John 14:5).

Jesus answers, "I am the way."

A few verses later Philip says, "Show us the Father" (John 14:8).

Jesus responds, "Don't you know me?"

That to me—and certainly to the people of his day—is the most incendiary truth-telling of all: a carpenter-rabbi from Nazareth declaring, "I am the truth" (John 14:6).

The Incarnation changes everything. The way is not just a set of directions or a collection of wisdom—it is a person. The truth is no longer just the correct doctrine or an airtight piece

The Incarnation changes everything. The way is not just a set of directions—it is a person. The truth is no longer just the correct doctrine—it is a person. The life is no longer just a biological fact—it is a person. "I am the Truth."

of evidence—it is a person. The life is no longer just a biological fact—it is a person.

I am the Truth.

～∾⌒∾～

Notice that at each stage of His arrest and trial, Jesus either spoke the truth or He remained silent because the questions mocked the truth. And for each truth He told, He suffered violence:

Before the soldiers and temple guards who arrested him
He told them, when they said they were looking for Jesus, "I am he" (John 18:5–8). The result: They tied Him up and led Him away.

Before Caiaphas, the high priest, and other teachers of the law
To their demand, "Tell us if you are the Christ, the Son of God," Jesus answered, "Yes, it is as you say" (Matthew 26:63–64). The result: They spit on Him and punched Him. When they did, He did not respond with retaliation, but with a piercing question: "If I spoke the truth, why do you strike me?" (John 18:23).

Before King Herod
Only three verses of Luke's account deal with the face-off between kings. King Herod wasn't really interested in getting truth from this "King of the Jews." He had only diversion and entertainment in mind. So he tried to get a rise out of Jesus—a king toying with the King. Jesus declined. The result: Herod ridiculed Him as a fraud, dressed Him up in royal attire, and sent Him back to Pilate as a walking joke.

Before Pilate
Pilate asked, "What is truth?" and then turned and walked away,

not waiting to hear the answer. Little did he know that the answer was standing before him, bloodied. The result: Even though Pilate found no reason to press charges against Jesus, he washed his hands of Him. He turned the Truth over to be flogged, and within hours, he condemned Him to be crucified.

Unfortunately, getting at the truth was not what any of these people were interested in.

∽

Telling the truth can be a serious and costly business. It cost Jesus His life, but at the same time, it purchased a new life for us. To be condemned means to forfeit all your freedom, but Jesus says that the truth means freedom (John 8:32).

And so the paradox remains: In this world the only true freedom comes from the truth of Jesus, and the inevitable consequence of testifying to the Truth is judgment by the world. To be free indeed, we must become slaves to the truth of Jesus. The condemnation that we will experience at all levels in the world is the truest freedom. Ask any one of the millions in prison in China, Sudan, Pakistan, Iraq, or Iran.

As Jesus hung on the cross, He quoted Psalm 31:5:

> *Into your hands I commit my spirit;*
> *redeem me, O LORD, the God of truth.*

How easily Christ could have escaped condemnation! After all, He knew what every question would be before it was asked. He had seen through every maneuver of His captors from the beginning of time.

But Jesus willingly let the authorities stamp *condemned* across the story of His life. He let Himself be condemned so that we could escape to new life in His name and look forward to an eternity enjoying forgiveness in His presence.

What the authorities in Jerusalem did not know that day was that truth would triumph. The Bible tells us exactly how....

A half-century later, the apostle John—friend of Jesus and eyewitness of the Incarnation—was given a vision of the future. John was a very old man by then, the last of the twelve disciples still alive. In his dream in the Spirit, a voice told him, "Write what you see..." (Revelation 1:11).

What he saw and recorded for us was not Jesus condemned by earthly powers, but Jesus coming again as majestic King of kings and Lord of lords. John saw Jesus not riding in on a borrowed donkey, but thundering back into history astride a magnificent white horse. "His eyes are like blazing fire," John wrote, "and on his head are many crowns "(Revelation 19:11–16)."

And what was this rider called? *Faithful and True.*

PRAYER

*Jesus, You were faithful to speak
the truth You heard from God,
But You died for it—a condemned man,
an enemy of the state,
a plaything for fools.
And You warned us that if they did these
things to You, we should be prepared for
the same kind of treatment.
Now, Master, prepare my heart with the truth.
I want to stand for truth today,
ready for prison if need be,
and waiting always in prayer with those
who suffer for You already.
Set me free from sin and
condemnation by Your grace,
and help me to know and love You more
—my faithful and true Lord.*

Amen

HE WAS CROWNED WITH THORNS
SO I MIGHT CROWN HIM WITH PRAISE

The soldiers twisted together a crown of thorns and put it on his head.

JOHN 19:2

For Jesus, the next scene is a coronation of shame, but for the Roman soldiers, the scene is just a game. At Pilate's orders, they strip off the purple robes that Herod had earlier draped around Him in sport and proceed to flog Jesus within an inch of His life. Jesus' entire back is torn and mangled. He staggers in a pool of His own blood. And now…the games begin.

"The soldiers twisted together a crown of thorns," John writes, "and put it on his head. They clothed him in a purple robe and went up to him again and again, saying 'Hail, king of the Jews!' And they struck him in the face" (John 19:2–3).

Like a crucifixion, the crowning with thorns was a particularly Roman aspect of the passion of Jesus.

Bronze crowns have been found in Canaan dating from before the time of Abraham, but the Roman crown was actually a wreath. The Romans had borrowed the tradition of bestowing honor through these lovely woven headpieces from the Greek athletic events held at Delphi and elsewhere. For example, at the Nemean games a wreath of oak leaves signified the winner. In Hellenistic times, vassal kings wore gilded wreaths as a sign of their authority. And Julius Caesar wore a wreath of laurels—the double message of both *winner* and *ruler* went well with his famous declaration of dominance: "I came. I saw. I conquered."

Crowns fashioned from plants were fairly common. What was unusual was the choice of thorns.

But for the soldiers' purposes, the choice was perfect. As a mocking symbol of "winner" and "ruler," the thorn wreath played to the public joke. And the spines, pressed down until they were embedded in Jesus' scalp, fed the soldiers' sick lust for inflicting pain.

⌘

While the torture is going on, Pilate comes out to address the raucous crowd. He tells them for the second time that he has found no basis for prosecuting Jesus. Just then the soldiers drag Jesus out onto the palace steps so the Jews can behold their king.

"Could that be Jesus?" one person whispers to another. Look! The hands that had healed them are bound. The head that bent over their children is pierced by spines. The face that lifted up thanks before feeding them by the thousands is streaked with blood.

Yes…it's Him! A purple mantle, matted darkly to His wounds, hangs off His shoulders and down His back.

"Ecce homo!" Pilate shouts. Here is the man!

The tone of Pilate's famous statement is not clear from the text. What does he mean? Is he joining the soldiers' mockery of Jesus? Or is he mocking the Jews for their dreams of independence? Is he actually trying to bring some balance to the proceeding by countering the soldiers' sarcastic claim that Jesus is king? Or is he even trying to arouse sympathy for Jesus?

Pilate's meaning may be unclear, but his deepest wish is not—he still fervently desires to be done with this nasty, no-win situation. I would interpret his declaration like this:

Soldiers pressed the spines down until they were embedded in Jesus' scalp.

"No, not *king!* Here is the *man!* Can't you see?"—pointing to the bloody wreath—"They're simple Judean *thorns!*"

But the chief priests and temple leaders won't have it. They start to chant, "Crucify! Crucify! Crucify!"

The mob picks up the rhythm: "Crucify! Crucify!"

Now Pilate abruptly changes his approach. "Behold your king!" he shouts. And signals to the soldiers to take Jesus away.

The mob wins.

❧

Yet Jesus is conquering.

Do you remember that as a penalty for the Fall, God cursed the earth with thorns? (Genesis 3:18). What had come freely and easily in the Garden would from then on be wrested from the soil through pain and sweat.

Now God's Son carries that curse on His head. The thorns also speak of wilderness (Judges 8:16), and Jesus, who knew the wilderness so well, now embarks on a journey. He will carry that twisted crown of shame into the wasteland of our sin. He will become lost there and forsaken.

Why?

To re-create and redeem this cursed world. Sinful man, who brought the kingdom of thorns down upon his own head, was helpless to save himself. But praise be to God! The one who wore those thorns like a crown *did* conquer the curse. The writer of Hebrews tells us Jesus is now "crowned with glory and honor because he suffered death, so that by the grace of God he might taste death for everyone" (Hebrews 2:9).

When Jesus appears at the end of time adorned with many crowns (Revelation 19:12), I hope and pray some of those crowns will be yours and mine. What better way to honor our King than to offer Him the crowns of righteousness He will give us in place of the wreath of shame we deserve.

That single thorny wreath replaced by a thousand radiant golden crowns! Those cries of "Crucify!" swallowed up forever in the roar of our praise.

It is the moment for which I long the most.

PRAYER

Master, I can still see You
crowned with thorns.
I can still hear the crowd jeering You.
Though I know today what they
could not have known,
still the humiliation stings.
Until the day I gratefully cast down
before You the crowns You have given me,
receive my thanks and praise.
Thank You for Your conquering grace
that broke the curse of sin
and took away my shame.
For the garments of dignity with which
You even now adorn me,
I thank You,
and I cast my worship at Your wounded feet.
Come, Lord Jesus.

Amen

HE WAS NAILED TO THE CROSS
SO I MIGHT ESCAPE JUDGMENT

And they crucified him.

MARK 15:24

Several years ago I was in China, walking along the top of the Great Wall. As I made my way along the wide path on top of the wall, my eyes swept the horizon. Then I began to notice something closer at hand: graffiti scribbled and carved on almost every rampart. In characters and languages from around the globe, visitors had left their marks to tell those who would come later, "Remember me—I was here!"

In an out-of-the-way spot, I noticed something carved into the soft stone. It was a cross. For some reason, I was startled. *How long has this cross been here?* I wondered. Perhaps for centuries. Chinese emperors had started building the Great Wall to keep out invaders three hundred years before Christ. Then an even more astonishing question came to my mind: *Could there be any corner on earth today where a*

person would not find some representation of the cross?

The worldwide sign of a suffering and a risen Savior has left its mark. On my heart. On my world.

Through it Jesus still says, "Remember me—I was here!"

⁂

The mock trials are over. The little that Pilate was willing to do to release Jesus, he has done. Now, for the record, he publicly washes his hands of the matter, as if the water could cleanse him of his responsibility. And then he utters the formal sentence: *"Ab in crucem."* You shall mount the cross.

Four soldiers carry out Jesus' execution. Although as many as six hundred men were sent to arrest Jesus, Pilate now sees little chance of a riot. Of all Jesus' supporters, only weeping women are left.

Two soldiers lift the forty-pound crossbeam onto Jesus' shoulders. He is going to carry His own cross to the place of execution. Around His neck hangs a piece of wood coated with white gypsum. Upon it, painted in black letters, is the crime with which He is charged. Dressed in cast-off purple, crowned with thorns, and labeled "King of the Jews," Jesus takes His first step as a condemned man. "Carrying his own cross," writes John, "he went out to the place of the Skull" (John 19:17).

Step by excruciating step, Jesus stumbles out of the Praetorium and down the twisted streets of the city, a great throng following. How far does He stagger before He falls face down and lies skinned and bruised beneath the beam?

Some onlookers turn their eyes from His agony. Others watch

disinterestedly while they hawk their wares, waiting for the mob to thin so they can carry on the real business of the day. Most cheer or curse as Jesus struggles to rise, takes another step, and stumbles past.

Soon He falls again. What makes Him crumple? Is it the weight of the crossbeam added to His wounds and loss of blood from the scourging? Is it the incalculable burden of the whole world's rebellion? Is it the weight of all our sorrows that presses Him down? It is all those things, and at last the weight grinds God's Son into the stones and stops the procession.

As Jesus lies exhausted on the ground, the soldiers search the crowd for someone to press into service. Under the Roman law of impressments, a soldier has the right to require anyone to carry a burden as far as one mile. Earlier, Jesus had told his followers that when they were faced with that demand, they should carry the burden two miles (Matthew 5:41).

The man they pick out of the crowd is named Simon. He is from Cyrene, the capital city of the North African district of Cyrenaica. Many Jews live there, and Simon has most likely come to celebrate Passover in the Cyrenian synagogue in Jerusalem (Acts 6:9). Mark and Luke both tell us he was on his way in from the country (Mark 15:21; Luke 23:26).

Simon shoulders the crossbeam and follows Jesus all the way to Golgotha. Then he disappears. Or does he? Mark identifies Simon as the father of Alexander and Rufus (Mark 15:21), and Paul greets a man named Rufus in his letter to the Romans (Romans 16:13). Mark assumes that his readers are acquainted with Simon's sons, so perhaps they are part of the fellowship in Rome. It is not difficult to imagine that Simon's experience so moved him that he became a follower of Jesus.

In the ancient world, crucifixion was considered the most severe form of capital punishment. In order of severity, decapitation was the least painful and was reserved for citizens of rank. Somewhere in the middle came being burned alive. Last came crucifixion, a fate reserved for slaves and criminals. Rulers particularly favored crucifixion when they wanted to make a public statement. "Whenever we crucify the guilty," wrote the Roman rhetorician Quintilian, "the most crowded roads are chosen, where the most people can see and be moved by this fear."

Three soldiers stretch Jesus out upon the crossbeam while the other picks up an iron spike. The nail is a tapered shaft from five to seven inches long. The fourth soldier swings his mallet high.

Romans did not invent death by crucifixion. Persians, Medes, Carthaginians, Assyrians, and Indians all practiced it in various forms. It probably began as a method of displaying the bodies of those who had been defeated in battle. As a warning to others who might be tempted to rebel, they impaled the conquered on poles or stakes. In fact, one of the Greek words for cross *(stauros)* originally described such stakes.

At some point, living victims began to be hung on poles or trees. Hence another Greek term for the cross is "tree" *(xulon)*. Eventually the crossbeam, or *patibulum*, was added. Sometimes an additional block of wood was nailed to the back of the cross to function as a saddle on which the victim could occasionally, although uncomfortably, rest. There is no evidence in the Gospels that this amenity was part of Jesus' crucifixion.

At Golgotha, the soldiers take the crossbeam from Simon's shoulders and place it at the foot of an upright timber that has been sunk securely into the rocky ground. The pole is one of three on the hill.

The crowd forms a tight, expectant circle around the site of the execution. Some spectators suddenly fall silent, and perhaps for the first time the wailing of the women can be heard.

Jesus is stripped of His outer garments, and they are divided among the four soldiers. The more expensive under-garment is set aside for later. They will gamble for this prize while they wait out their victims' final hours (Psalm 22:18; Luke 23:34).

Now three soldiers stretch Jesus out upon the crossbeam while the other picks up an iron spike. The nail is a tapered shaft from five to seven inches long and about three-eights of an inch across.

The fourth soldier swings his mallet high. The women turn away. The mallet falls, pounding the spike through Jesus' flesh and deep into wood. Seconds later, the second spike is pounded home. Now Jesus is impaled on the crossbeam.

The soldiers hoist up the beam on which Jesus hangs bleeding and fasten it to the upright timber. With the crossbeam in place, the soldiers grasp Jesus' feet and place them one on top of the other. Next they hold a piece of wood over His crossed feet and drive a single spike through it, through His heel bones, and into the wood of the cross.

The sentence for Jesus has been carried out. The soldiers turn their attention to two manacled thieves. All that lies ahead for Jesus is agony and waiting.

Crucifixion was death by exhaustion—every minute consumed with the painful necessity of struggling to suck in another breath. In fact, medical experts tell us that David's cry in Psalm 69 is a physiologically accurate description of Jesus' experience of dying. "Save me, O God, for the waters have come up to my neck. I sink in the miry depths, where there is no foothold" (vv. 1–2).

The legacy of death by crucifixion is still with us in the word "excruciating," which literally means "out of the cross." To extend the life—and thus the torment—of the victim, the executioners took care not to damage his vital organs. If they performed everything properly, he could hang for as long as nine days before death finally came.

If they had flogged the victim repeatedly beforehand, however, he could die sooner from loss of blood. This could help to explain the unusual fact that Jesus died on the same day He was crucified. When Joseph of Arimathea came to claim the body, Pilate was amazed that Jesus had died so quickly—only six hours after He had been nailed to the cross (Mark 15:44).

⌁

Can you see Him? Jesus hangs between heaven and earth. His blood seeps into the rough timbers and drips to the ground. To breathe, He must heave Himself up by His impaled hands and feet so that His lungs can expand. This is no idealized scene from a Renaissance painting.

The upright timber at His back points to heaven and the Father, but the Father has turned away. The timber also points down to earth and mankind, but rulers of men want Jesus dead.

The crossbeam to which His hands are nailed reaches out on one side to embrace a criminal who will find redemption, and on the other side to invite a lawbreaker who will spurn it.

At the precise spot where the upright and the crossbeam meet beats the living heart of Jesus.

"Now is the time for judgment on this world," Jesus had said earlier that week. "Now the prince of this world will be driven out. But I, when I am lifted up from the earth, will draw all men to myself" (John 12:31–32).

Judgment on the world? Draw all men to Himself? If I had been watching the cross-beams go up on Golgotha that day, I would have decided that Jesus was wrong. There is the proof: He hangs alone, scorned and humiliated, awaiting the most miserable of deaths. Yet if I had been looking back across the centuries—over generations, cultures, and my own life transformed by this crucified Christ—I would know He was right. It was time for judgment.

With every blow of the mallet, the judgment of the world fell on just one man.

But with every blow of the mallet, the judgment of the world fell on just one man. "Christ redeemed us from the curse of the law by becoming a curse for us," wrote Paul. "For it is written: 'Cursed is everyone who is hung on a tree'" (Galatians 3:13).

Hanging there between heaven and earth, Jesus became the sole reconciling force between God and every human being who would ever live. With His own blood, Jesus paid the penalty for our sins and drew us all back under the covering of grace.

The cross.

Today, if your eyes should fall upon that precious symbol, remember:

Jesus was here. And He was lifted up for you.

PRAYER

O Lord, You suffered the judgment of death on the cross
so I might live free of the penalty for my own sins.
Give me the grace to live a life worthy of Your great sacrifice.
By Your Spirit, allow me to stand before Your cross every day,
continually experiencing afresh
the wonder of Your forgiveness and the depth of Your love.
Loving Savior, You have drawn me to Yourself.
May Your remarkable demonstration of love
be revealed in my life today,
drawing all men and women to You.

Amen

HE WAS STRETCHED OUT
BETWEEN THIEVES
SO I COULD KNOW THE REACH OF LOVE

> *He poured out his life unto death,*
> *and was numbered with the transgressors.*
> *For he bore the sin of many, and made*
> *intercession for the transgressors.*

ISAIAH 53:12B

*H*e had always been a troublemaker, it seems—a criminal, a rebel, an unwanted specimen of humanity. And two thousand years later, the repentant thief who died with Jesus is still making trouble. Some people—especially very religious ones—protest that Jesus was too soft on him, too forgiving, as He was with the woman taken in adultery. Others have used the story of the thief to argue about baptism. I once heard a preacher say that regardless of what Jesus said about being with Him in paradise, the repentant thief could not have been saved since he "never got wet."

But then, it is in the nature of criminals to make trouble.

Exactly who were the two thieves who died with Jesus? In the absence of personal information in the Gospels, ancient

11

Three new crosses broke the skyline. On the left hung a criminal. On the right, another criminal. And in between, His arms spread out to each, hung the Son of God.

manuscripts have filled in the gaps with names like Dysmas and Gestas, Joathas and Maggatras, Capnatas and Gamatras, Zoathem and Camma. But these are most likely guesswork or fiction.

We don't know the details of their crimes, either, since we find no mention of titular inscriptions above their heads. John refers to them simply and perhaps generously as "two others."

From Matthew and Mark, we learn that they were robbers or bandits. Yet because in Roman law robbery was not punishable by death, the charge that brought them to Golgotha must have been more serious than an incident or two of lawbreaking. Perhaps they had been bandits by profession. Or perhaps they had been jailed along with Barabbas for taking part in the insurrection mentioned in Mark 15:7.

Luke's account of the two thieves is his longest and most significant addition to the crucifixion narrative. As concerned as he was to emphasize Jesus' innocence, Luke may have chosen to portray the two guilty men in more detail in order to highlight the contrast between them and Jesus.

Whoever the two men were and whatever their crime, three men received the sentence of death that day. Three were flogged. Three stumbled out of the city, carrying crosses, guarded by soldiers, and followed by tormenting crowds.

When the three arrived together at Golgotha, an awful sight might have greeted them. Earlier victims—dying or long since dead—may still have been hanging, since it was customary to display the corpses of those crucified. In the third century A.D. one witness wrote, "Punished with limbs outstretched, they are fastened and nailed to the stake in the most bitter torment, evil food for birds of prey and grim picking for dogs."

Guilt or innocence notwithstanding, the Place of the Skull received the three men with grim indifference. The soldiers raised the mallets with the same brute force and drove the spikes through the flesh with equal finality.

When the job was done, three new crosses broke the skyline. On the left hung a criminal. On the right, another criminal. And in between, His arms spread out to each, hung the Son of God.

∽∾

The three crosses have been raised and the clamor of the crowd has subsided. The earlier screams of the two dying thieves have given way to groans and curses.

Now they turn to the silent man between them, trying to find some relief from their own misery by tormenting Jesus. "Those crucified with him also heaped insults on him," wrote Mark (Mark 15:32).

"Aren't you the Christ?" gasps one. "Save yourself and us!" (Luke 23:39).

But somehow, one of the criminals has a sudden change of heart. Perhaps when he heard the soldiers mocking Jesus, calling him "King," something in his heart softened and broke. Maybe the profane ranting of the other thief threw into stark relief the gulf between his own guilt and the silent

Was the criminal's desire for salvation driven only by fear? Was it a pain-crazed plea from between clenched teeth? Or was it sincere leap of faith based on sudden contrition?

man's innocence. With his next breath, he rebukes the other criminal.

"Don't you fear God since you are under the same sentence?" he asks. "We are punished justly, for we are getting what our deeds deserve. But this man has done nothing wrong" (Luke 23:40–41).

And then a miracle happens. The thief turns to Jesus. "Jesus," he pleads, "remember me when you come into your kingdom" (Luke 23:42).

With these words, an unnamed thief becomes the only one we know of to speak to Jesus on the cross without derision or mockery. An unnamed thief is the only person in the Bible who calls Jesus by His personal name, without any kind of title attached, as if their mutual suffering has placed them on an intimate, first-name basis. In so doing, he becomes the first to address Jesus the way most of us do today. And with his words, that unnamed thief becomes the first to be drawn to the crucified Christ.

Jesus answers with a guarantee. "Today you will be with me in paradise" (Luke 23:43).

❦

Paradise—it is one of the oldest words in our language. For centuries it has maintained its basic consonantal form, *prds*. In Hebrew it is *pardes*; in Greek, *paradeisos*. The best we can tell, it is an ancient Persian form that originally referred to a walled garden. The word appears two other times in the New Testament. In 2 Corinthians 12:4, Paul speaks of the vision in which, whether in his body or out of it—he is not sure—he went to paradise and heard "inexpressible things." In the same passage he also calls this place "the third heaven." In Revelation 2:7, John says he heard Jesus use the word to describe the place where the tree of life grows.

Was the criminal's desire for salvation driven only by fear? Was it a pain-crazed plea from between clenched teeth? Or was it a sincere leap of faith based on sudden contrition?

We don't know. The sentence could easily have been the first prayer of an entirely misspent life. But the thief asked only once—and needed to ask only once. The Son of God looked over at him and gave him his answer: "Today...."

A few hours later, Jesus died.

The thieves clung to life for several hours more. When the soldiers saw that they were still alive, they picked up heavy mallets and broke their legs. No longer able to lift up and draw air into their lungs, the two survivors started a grotesque dance, a losing battle with suffocation. Soon, they too hung still and lifeless against the sky.

But one of them awoke in paradise.

∽◯∽

Those criminals perfectly represent all humankind. Like them, we have all sinned. Like them, we all deserve only death.

Like one of them, many people today will refuse hope, rejecting the possibility that Jesus could really be King. The love, mercy, forgiveness, eternal life, and paradise He offers—all will seem impossible, unbelievable, unreachable, unacceptable.

But some will receive all, simply by asking.

Jesus was stretched out on that cross between criminals so

that we can know for ourselves the amazing reach of His love. From every wasted life, from every compromised motive, from every personal hell—it reaches all the way to paradise.

PRAYER

Dear Jesus, You answered in love
the thief crucified beside You.
Answer me, I pray.
You remembered him; remember me this day.
I, too, have been a rebel from birth.
In my coveting I have stolen, and
in my anger I have murdered.
I deserve punishment no less than that dying thief.
So look on the one You love and died for.
Remember me in Your mercy so that I may
deeply know and faithfully express Your love—
and live forever with You in paradise.

Amen

HE SUFFERED THIRST
SO I CAN DRINK LIVING WATER

"I am thirsty."

JOHN 19:28

According to the Gospels, Jesus spoke seven times while He was hanging on the cross. Since the process of crucifixion eventually caused the victim to suffocate, we can understand the extreme effort it took for Him to speak at all. As we would expect, all His utterances were short, presumably gasping phrases.

Jesus must have said, "I am thirsty" only seconds after he shouted, "My God, my God, why have You forsaken me?"

No wonder He was parched. Besides the dehydrating effects of severe blood loss, Jesus had endured the spiritual travail of three hours of darkness and separation from His Father.

Yet Jesus' statement was more than an indication of His

need. It was the fulfillment of the final prophesy about the Passion. He said it "so that the Scripture would be fulfilled" (John 19:28). That Scripture is found in Psalm 69:

> *I looked for sympathy, but there was none,*
> *for comforters, but I found none.*
> *They put gall in my food*
> *and gave me vinegar for my thirst.*

(20–21)

The prophecy was fulfilled precisely. The soldiers soaked a sponge in wine vinegar and lifted it to His lips on a stalk. This vinegar was a cheap soured wine that Roman soldiers often drank on duty to keep awake.

Earlier, some compassionate women of Jerusalem had offered Him a mixture of wine and myrrh to help deaden the pain, but Jesus had refused it. He would not go into His Passion with His senses dulled by narcotics. He asked for a drink only when His suffering was complete. The end was near.

I wonder if a certain woman moved furtively at the edges of the murderous crowd that day. A Samaritan, she would have been cautious about making her presence known in the city during Passover. Once during a conversation that began with His request for water, this amazing rabbi had changed her life. Is it possible that she had come to Jerusalem a few days earlier to hail Him as King and that she now kept a forlorn vigil as He was crucified? Perhaps.

"Will you give me a drink?" He had asked her that day by the village well. The question startled her—good Jews were far too religious to even touch the water jars of Samaritans. In return He offered her living water. His gift for her soul-thirst would become in her, He said, "a spring of water welling up to eternal life" (John 4:14). Only later had she realized that Jesus' thirst was both the means and the opportunity for her to experience lifelong satisfaction.

I wonder, too, how those other faithful women who waited near the cross received Jesus' words. Surely they remembered the time in Jerusalem when He stood up on the last day of the Feast of Tabernacles. The high priest had just quoted from Isaiah: "With joy you will draw water from the wells of salvation!" (12:3). The moment the priest poured water out of the golden pitcher in front of the throng, a voice rang out. It was Jesus.

"Whoever drinks the water I give him will never thirst. Indeed, the water I give him will become in him a spring of water welling up to eternal life."

JOHN 4:14

"If anyone is thirsty, let him come to me and drink," He declared to the surprised crowd (John 7:37). And then He repeated his dramatic promise: "Whoever believes in me, as the Scripture has said, streams of living water will flow from within him" (v. 38).

Pure, life-giving water—bubbling up, flowing out in never-ending streams, washing over dry lips, quenching the most desperate thirst—free for whoever believes. The Feast of Tabernacles celebrated God's provision of water from the rock in the wilderness, and Jesus wanted everyone to know that it had arrived. This time God had sent Living Water, but first the Rock must be struck.

And now on that ugly hill, the one who spoke those hope-filled words was gasping through cracked lips, "I am thirsty."

Jesus' tormenting thirst on the cross was only part of the

agony He suffered for you and me. But by a mysterious exchange, He became the Living Water who experienced unquenchable thirst. Why? Now, by the power of the Holy Spirit, a follower of Jesus need never again experience soul-thirst (John 4:14).

Now also, from each of us, a refreshing stream can flow—pure, life-giving, and free. Through my hands, your voice, and our very presence on this thirsty planet, Jesus still extends His offer:

"Come to me and drink."

PRAYER

Jesus, source of the true, living water,
so often I am thirsty for You.
But how can this be?
You said that I would never be
thirsty again if I came to You.
Could it be that I do not come to You as I should?
That I "dig my own cisterns"?
If this is so, Lord, forgive me.
Let this thirst draw me to You.
Let nothing else satisfy, even for a second,
so that, in return, I might provide for a thirsty world
the only Water that satisfies forever.

Amen

HE SAID, "IT IS FINISHED"
SO I COULD BEGIN MY WALK OF FAITH

*"My food," said Jesus, "is to do
the will of him who sent me
and to finish his work."*

JOHN 4:34

*B*y now you may have noticed that the chronology of certain events of the crucifixion must be inferred by comparing the accounts in the Gospels. Since they seem to have somewhat different purposes and intended audiences, each author writes from a slightly different perspective. For example, only Luke records Jesus' promise to the repentant thief. The need for comparison applies to Jesus' words from the cross, too.

What were His last words? Both Matthew and Mark report that before Jesus was offered the wine vinegar, He cried out with a loud voice, "My God, my God, why have you forsaken me?" and then expired (Matthew 27:46, 50; Mark 15:34, 37).

Luke skips ahead from the account of the thieves to noon,

13

when darkness fell for three hours. He reports that, after that fearful time had passed,

> Jesus called out with a loud voice, "Father, into
> your hands I commit my spirit." When he had said this,
> he breathed his last.

(LUKE 23:46)

In this exclamation from the cross, Jesus has reverted from the more formal tone of "My God, my God..." to the familiar and personal form of addressing God as His Father. Here again His words are those of the psalmist who prophetically quotes Jesus:

> Into your hands I commit my spirit;
> redeem me, O LORD, the God of truth.

(PSALM 31:5)

All of the synoptic Gospels tell us that Jesus shouted His final words. And something about His final declaration caught the attention of the centurion in charge. The career Roman soldier was clearly impressed. How many crucified men he must have seen dying as pathetic or profane cowards! Yet this one—vilified and mocked more than any—endured dying with dignity and met death not with a whimper, but with a shout of victory. "Surely this man was the Son of God," the centurion exclaimed (Mark 15:39). Luke even records that the soldier, pagan until that moment, gave praise to God (Luke 23:47).

Jesus bled and died like any other man, but *how* He died proved He was more than a man. He turned every experience of violence into a demonstration of divine power.

The results? *Even during the violence, grace triumphed.* First the thief dying alongside Jesus was won into the kingdom. Then the very soldier who carried out the sentence was won—and moved to worship!

⋙ ⋘

John, more than any other Gospel writer, saw Jesus as God's Son, sent to earth to do God's work. "We must do the work of him who sent me," Jesus had told his disciples (John 9:4). The night before His crucifixion, He had prayed, "I have brought you glory on earth by completing the work you gave me to do" (John 17:4). So it's not surprising that the last words of Jesus that John recorded put Jesus' suffering in the context of work completed:

> When he had received the drink, Jesus said, "It is finished." With that, he bowed his head and gave up his spirit.

(JOHN 19:30)

Since John's Gospel tells us that Jesus "said" these final words, I think it's reasonable to conclude that this utterance is not the final "loud cry" of Matthew and Luke. John is careful with details like these.

"It is finished" is certainly an enigmatic final testimony. Scholars have speculated about what that little word—"it"—referred to. What task was finished? The word could convey several meanings:

How many crucified men the centurion must have seen dying as pathetic or profane cowards! Yet this one— vilified and mocked more than any— endured dying with dignity and met death not with a whimper, but with a shout of victory.

- The ordeal of suffering had run its course.
- The prophecies of Scripture had been fulfilled.
- The rule of law as a basis for meeting God's approval had been abolished.
- Jesus' earthly life had reached an end.

Most certainly, Jesus' words meant that the Father's work He had come to do was finally done. All the violence of the world's sin had been placed upon one person, God's Son. The penalty had been fully paid. The tyranny of sin had been toppled. The whole work of winning salvation for us had been accomplished—no human being could add even one thing to it.

Job done!

Note that Jesus did not say, "It is over." The wonderful truth is that Jesus' work of redemption was just beginning in the lives of His followers. Now it was time for the disciples—most of whom at that moment were cowering behind locked doors—to take their stand.

$$\infty$$

To the disciples, at first it must have seemed a daunting task to carry on with Jesus' work. But He had prepared them. He had taught them and walked with them through every situation they would face in serving Him. Consider how Mark shows all they had been through in the process of preparation. They had been "with Jesus":

- as He taught and healed the multitude (3:7–12);
- as He faced rejection from His own family as well as the

religious leaders (3:20–35);
- as He confronted the demoniac (4:35–5:20);
- in the face of disease and death (5:21–43);
- in the face of personal rejection (6:1–6).

Only then did He commission and send them out (6:12-13).

With time the disciples would realize that Jesus never called them to do anything He had not already done, including the laying down of His life. And now by the power of the Holy Spirit, they could set about the work of spreading the Good News. If the burden of their ministry became confusing or overwhelming, they could remember Jesus' simple definition of the job at hand: "The work of God is this: to believe in the one he has sent" (John 6:29).

That was the whole task—to live a life wholly defined and motivated by belief in Him. Everything else they accomplished for the kingdom, not matter how great or small, would flow from this.

❧

Jesus showed us what this work of believing in Him looks like: He totally depended on the Father every minute of His earthly life, and He totally surrendered His will to the Father's will.

We can't do the work of Jesus. Only He could bring us the extravagant riches of His grace—forgiveness, healing, salvation, and eternal life. That work is accomplished, complete in every detail—*finished!*

But we can determine, with grateful and obedient hearts, to finish the work of belief He has given us to do. Jesus has prepared us for carrying out our mission. Through the Scriptures we have been "with Him" in every situation, every ordeal, so that we, too, can go about our lives transformed. Out of a simple, powerful belief in Jesus Christ, our ministry—which is, after all, His ministry—can flow.

Do we really *believe* in our crucified, yet triumphant Lord? Are we working a complete and radical faith in Him into every moment, every priority of our day?

Like Jesus, not until our last breath on earth will we be able to say of our true life's work, "It is finished."

PRAYER

Lord, thank You for finishing Your work of bringing
to our world life, hope,
and freedom from the penalty of sin.
I praise You, and I believe in You.
Please search out any unbelief You find in me.
Help me to see that it is You who are
so powerfully working in me.
And help me to understand that believing is pointless
unless You are the sole object of my belief.
By Your grace and power,
I want to go about my work for Your kingdom today
in total dependence on the Father.

Amen

HE WAS GOD'S LAMB, SLAIN
SO I COULD CLAIM HIS SACRIFICE AS MY OWN

*Christ, our Passover lamb,
has been sacrificed.*

1 CORINTHIANS 5:7

*S*uppose the New Testament writers could have used only one word to describe Jesus' fate on the cross. What would it have been? Lynched? Killed? Murdered? Executed?

All those words are true to some degree, but they do not convey the grandest truth. Jesus met His death in all those ways, but the real meaning of His death is conveyed in another word. Jesus was *sacrificed*. His death was about making amends for something that had gone terribly wrong. He gave up His life as a substitute offering to pay for and take away the sins of the world.

God offered Jesus' life. Jesus willingly gave it up. "Sacrifice" is the only word that conveys both the horror and the glory of Calvary.

Judaism in its original state was a bloody affair. It is one

125

thing for pastors today to speak of Christ being a substitution-ary sacrifice and a propitiation for our sins. It was another for a priest in Jesus' day to lay hold of a soft white lamb and slit its throat. Yet Christianity began on the altar, in an inconceivably violent incident we call the crucifixion.

It would be a travesty to talk about the violence of the cru-cifixion without remembering that Jesus, as He hung on the cross, was not only the dying Son of God, but also the slain Lamb of God.

∽∾

For Jesus, it began the night He was born. The first to come and kneel at His manger were shepherds. He arrived in the season when lambs were being born—that's why the shepherds were in the fields all night. The worshiping shepherds saw a baby boy sweetly sleeping, bur they never expected that the lamb who was born that night as a baby was the Lamb of God.

Thirty years later, John the Baptist was standing up to his waist in the Jordan when he saw Jesus approaching. "Look!" he exclaimed. "The Lamb of God who takes away the sin of the world!" With those words ringing through the air, Jesus began three years of public ministry.

John spoke more than he knew. Prophets usually do. But Jesus knew, even then, that in order to take the sin of the world away He must take it upon Himself and, like a lamb, be sacrificed.

I wonder if one of the last sounds to reach Jesus' ears during the final hours on the cross was the bleating of lambs. After all, people by the score were still streaming past Golgotha on their way into Jerusalem for Passover. Many of them would have herded before them their families' finest, whitest lambs, which, like Jesus, had been set aside for sacrifice.

Those families walking into Jerusalem that day saw a blood-ied man hanging on a cross by the side of the road. They didn't know He was also a lamb. They couldn't know that He was changing everything—that the old order was passing away and that the book of the law, along with its complex and highly sym-bolic system of sacrifices, was about to slam shut—because God had stepped up to the altar and, like Abraham, provided His own Son as the sacrificial Lamb.

∽◦◦

On the evening of the crucifixion, some priests working in the temple began talking. It had occurred to one of them that it might not be a good idea for Passover visitors to see three crucifixions in progress. Usually vic-tims' bodies were left to rot or be consumed by crows. But tomorrow was a special Sabbath, and that wouldn't do. Besides, Jesus had caused enough trouble already, and they did not want Passover crowds to turn Him into a martyr.

One of the last sounds to reach Jesus' ears during the final hours on the cross was the bleating of lambs.

Certain that all three men must still be alive, they sent word of their predicament to Pilate. The priests knew the Romans some-times hastened the deaths of the crucified by breaking their legs. So the priests asked Pilate to have the legs of all three broken so that the bodies could be taken down before morning.

By then Pilate must have been impressed with the priests' ability to sway public opinion. He agreed.

When the soldiers returned to Golgotha, the thieves were still alive, writhing for each breath. Probably with the same mallet they had used to drive the spikes through Jesus' flesh earlier in the day, the soldiers now smashed the victims' legs. But when they came to Jesus, they saw no need.

They saw only a motionless form, a colorless face. They didn't know He was the Lamb of God, slain. Or that in the book of Exodus, among the minute instructions on how to sacrifice the Passover lamb, was the statement: "Do not break any of the bones" (Exodus 12:46). Or that David had written: "He protects all his bones, not one of them will be broken" (Psalm 34:20).

Writing his Gospel decades later, John was still amazed. "The man who saw it has given testimony, and his testimony is true," he wrote. "These things happened so that the Scripture would be fulfilled, 'Not one of his bones will be broken'" (John 19:35–36).

∽∾

When complicated theological truths begin to overwhelm you, try focusing your attention on this one truth: *Jesus Christ is God's Lamb, slain for me.* Read the book of Revelation, for more than any other book of the Bible, it speaks about Jesus as the Lamb of God. For example, John writes:

- *Then I saw a Lamb, looking as if it had been slain. (5:6)*
- *In a loud voice they sang: "Worthy is the Lamb, who was slain." (5:12)*

> *To him who sits on the throne and to the Lamb be praise and honor and glory and power, for ever and ever! (5:13)*

> *Then I looked, and there before me was the Lamb, standing on Mount Zion. (14:1)*

> *I did not see a temple in the city, because the Lord God Almighty and the Lamb are its temple. The city does not need the sun or the moon to shine on it, for the glory of God gives it light, and the Lamb is its lamp. (21:22–23)*

Every time a Jewish man watched the priest slaughter a sacrificial lamb for him and his family, he knew that an innocent, beautiful creature was taking their place—suffering the fate they should have suffered for their sins. There could be no escaping the awareness that the magnitude of their sin required such a death. Just before the sacrifice, the worshiper who presented the lamb laid both of his hands on it. By his touch, he signified that he understood the exchange: *What happens to the lamb should have happened to me.*

Jesus Christ is God's Lamb for you and me. And as we come to the cross, let us come humbly, laying trembling hands upon the Lamb. He will hear us whisper through our tears: "What happened to you, Lord Jesus, should have happened to me."

Let us remember, too, that one day—and for all eternity thereafter—this sinless, spotless Lamb who was slain will reign—receiving all praise, honor, glory, and power.

PRAYER

Lord Jesus, You who are the spotless Lamb,
upon whom I lay my hands,
hear my praise,
joining with those redeemed
from every corner of the world
and from all time, forever,
saying:
"Worthy is the Lamb,
worthy is the Lamb,
most worthy is the Lamb!"

Amen

HE WAS FORSAKEN BY THE FATHER
SO I WOULD NEVER BE REJECTED

*"My God, my God,
why have you forsaken me?"*

MATTHEW 27: 46

*H*ave you experienced the feeling of being cut off from someone you love? Cast aside by someone you thought would always be there for you? Abandoned by heaven just when your life seemed to be descending into hell? Then you know what it feels like to be forsaken.

Not too long ago, my best friend and I drifted apart. We had both been too busy for too long a period of time; I was on the road, and he was consumed with ministry at home. Days turned into weeks and then into months. At last the time came when we had almost no contact. I had started attending another church from where my friend ministered when the Lord graciously intervened.

One day, when we both ended up in the same mens group,

15

my friend made a comment about my changing churches. For me it was a painful stab. A few days later, I went to his office to talk. It took a half an hour or so of tiptoeing around the issue before we could get to the real problem: We both felt that the other had abandoned the friendship. I figured he'd written me off; he thought I couldn't care less about him.

After sincere apologies were given and received, our relationship was restored.

To understand Jesus' experience of separation from the Father on the cross, we could begin with theology, but I would rather start with relationship. Everyone fears abandonment—we feel it keenly in our hearts.

Talk about relationship! Jesus and His Father were truly inseparable. Jesus had told His disciples, "I and the Father are one" (John 10:30). And when the Father had presented His only Son to the world, He had thundered from heaven, "This is my Son, whom I love; with him I am well pleased" (Matthew 3:17).

But when darkness descended on the cross that afternoon at Calvary, a Grand Canyon of separation yawned open between them. For the first time in all of eternity, Jesus was alone. Abandoned. No Father. No answers. Only silence.

⁂

In Gethsemane, Jesus had castigated Judas and the others, "This is your hour—when darkness reigns" (Luke 22:53). What a long hour it became!

At noon on the day of Jesus' crucifixion, "Darkness came over the whole land until the ninth hour, for the sun stopped shining" (Luke 23:44–45).

Without warning, a loathsome blackness descended. Suddenly, the brightest lights in the city were the sacrificial fires burning in the temple courtyard. We can imagine the terror that accompanied such unexplained and total blackness—people scrambling for candles, lamps, and torches; mothers huddling indoors, clutching their children. *Would the sun ever return?* they wondered. *Was this the end of the world?* Surely the darkness felt like a sentence of doom.

Scholars love to debate the cause of the darkness. Some argue, for example, that Luke uses a word to describe the event that can be translated "eclipse." But we know from astronomy that when the moon is full, as it always is for Passover, a total eclipse is impossible.

In any case, it seems to me that they miss the point. Do we debate how Jesus walked on the water? Both miracles are clues to the relationship that exists between Jesus and Creation. Through Jesus, God made Creation, and through Him, God sustains it (Colossians 1:15–17; Hebrews 1:3). Jesus can walk on the waters because He is Lord over the waters. At the moment of His death, the light of the sun died because its Sustainer was dying as well.

No wonder startled Jews saw signs above and felt earthquakes below (Matthew 27:51–53). I suspect the ripples of a shaken Creation radiated out from that cross past planets and stars to the farthest ends of the universe. And they may be radiating still.

Jesus had told His disciples, "I and the Father are one." But when darkness descended on the cross Jesus was alone. Abandoned. No Father. No answers. Only silence.

In Exodus chapter 10, God told Moses, "Stretch out your hand toward the sky so that darkness will spread over Egypt—*darkness that can be felt.*" Why? Because the darkness then, as at Golgotha, was a sign that God's curse rested upon the land. Except for the homes of the Israelites, Egypt was in darkness for three days.

This was the ninth plague. As you might remember, the tenth and final one took firstborn sons. But God told His people that if they would sacrifice a lamb and mark the doorposts of their houses with its blood, the angel of death would not enter that house—he would "pass over."

Now centuries later, the Israelites had gathered in Jerusalem to celebrate Passover and remember how God had provided for their ancestors. Yet as they made preparations for the memorial meal or carried their own lambs to the temple for sacrifice, they did not know that God was in the process of making an even greater provision. On a hill outside the city walls, God was sacrificing His own firstborn, His spotless Lamb. The blood of Jesus would forever mark the doorposts of the hearts of those who would come to believe in Him.

∞

The ancient creeds of the church say that Jesus descended into hell. Hell is the price of sin. A good description of hell might be that it is a place where the absence of God feels like the most oppressive burden imaginable. During those hours on Golgotha, Jesus descended there—into hell, the labyrinthine darkness of total abandonment by the Father.

How could it be any other way? Jesus had taken upon Himself the past, present, and future sin of the whole world. He had traded His beauty for the ugliness of our sin.

But God is holy; God is light. "In him there is no darkness at all," wrote John (1 John 1:5). His eyes are "too pure to look on evil" (Habakkuk 1:13). And so the eyes of the Father turned away from His own Son, and the darkness descended.

The first words from Jesus' lips as He was coming out of that black silence reveal the state of His heart. He cried out with a loud voice, "My God, why have you forsaken me?"

The scholar Alfred Edersheim tells us that at the ninth hour—precisely at the moment of this cry—a three fold blast of the shofar would have sounded from the temple to announce the close of the evening service. Perhaps the harsh notes of the ram's horn over the ramparts of Jerusalem mingled with Jesus' forsaken cry. One sound represented the old order that was passing away; the other, the new that was about to commence.

"My God, my God, why...?" may be the most painful question any human can ask.

Jesus' question, the only expression from the cross that appears in more than one Gospel, is spoken in a garbled Aramaic and Hebrew phrase: *"Eloi, Eloi, lama sabachthani?"* (Mark 15:34). The words are from Psalm 22:1. The fact the Jesus mixed two languages might have been a sign of the extremity of His suffering. As physically excruciating as the scourging, the nails, the thorns, and the cross were, and as emotionally humiliating as the mockery was, the spiritual desolation Jesus had experienced in that oppressive darkness and silence must have been the most painful aspect of the cross.

"My God, my God, why…?"

It may be the most painful question any human can ask. Often, at its most visceral level, it is not a request for information so much as a howl of anguish. As far as we know, it was the only time Jesus ever asked his Father, "Why?"

"My God, my God, why…?"

You and I know the answer: Jesus was forsaken at Golgotha because of our sin. Now, because of the redemption Jesus purchased for us in darkness, we can live forever in God's light. Because of the separation He endured for us, we—who have so often turned our back on our Father—have the guarantee that He will never forsake us.

You and I can go through our day today with complete confidence that our Father's eyes are always toward us. Covered as we are by grace, He sees us as His adopted and wholly beautiful sons and daughters.

❧

PRAYER

Lord, Jesus, King of the kingdom of light,
though my feelings would lie
and sometimes tell me otherwise,
my faith shouts that You will never leave me in the dark.
You endured the darkness that was
totally other, completely unlike You,
so that I might never be in nor even fear the darkness.
Today, because of Your redeeming grace,
I can flourish in my Father's promise:
"Never will I leave you; never will I forsake you."
Blessings, thanks, praise to You!

Amen

HE CHOSE THE SHAME
OF WEAKNESS
SO I CAN KNOW THE HOPE OF GLORY

*Who for the joy set before
him endured the cross,
scorning its shame.*

HEBREWS 12:2

"*K*eep an eye on the one in the middle," some onlooker might have said that day. "He's the one to watch. You never know what might happen."

Words like these might have come from a boy with nothing better to do than squat on that stony hill and watch. Or from a man who had known Lazarus before he died—and had talked with him after this Jesus had brought him back to life. Or from a woman who had been healed by His touch. Or from a synagogue teacher still fearful that this upstart rabbi from Galilee might yet make fools of the whole religious establishment.

16

Until His corpse was laid to rest, there was always the *possibility* that at the last moment this Jesus could call upon those legions of angels He had said were at His command.

The apostle John and a handful of women watched and waited, too. How their hearts ached with grief, yet still clung to hope. Was Jesus truly King of kings? Then how could a city full of priests and soldiers thwart His will? Was He their long-awaited Messiah? Then how could any Roman power overcome Him? Wasn't He truly God? Then how could three nails hold Him? At any moment, something could happen....

But nothing happened.

No angelic intervention.

No reply.

No miracle.

By the end of that afternoon, it appeared to doubters and believers alike that Jesus had completely and utterly failed to prove His claims. The nails pounded His failure into wood. The thorns etched it in flesh. The blood colored it in pools of dark, coagulated red.

The angels and the shepherds had been wrong.

The wise men had obviously been fools.

John the Baptist, his head full of visions and prophecy, must have heard some other voice in the wilderness.

All those miracles must have been mere sleight of hand.

And of all the things He had said He was, Jesus' claim to be the Son of God now seemed the most impossible of all.

On this hill, every hope for the crucified Jesus had ended in shame and weakness.

∽∾

Jesus' surrender to weakness started, paradoxically, with a prayer for glory. "Father, the time has come," He had prayed the night before in the upper room. "Glorify your Son, that your Son may glorify you" (John 17:1).

Glory was much on His mind that night. He knew the horror that awaited Him the next day, yet He used the word "glory" eight times in His prayer. He asked for glory for Himself and for His disciples.

John, who heard the prayer and recorded it for us years later, can be forgiven for not entertaining the prospect of glory by the close of that day on Golgotha. I do not find the slightest indication in the text of the Gospels that anyone sensed it. Only a madman could witness such a spectacle of weakness and shame and declare, "Glory!"

> *Only a madman could witness such a spectacle of weakness and shame and declare, "Glory!"*

But later, after God had given the disciples eyes of faith, they saw past the violence of the cross to the glory that Christ had won there. "We were eyewitnesses to his majesty," wrote Peter (2 Peter 1:16). "We have seen his glory," wrote John (John 1:14).

To win glory for us, Jesus willingly remained on the cross, refusing to use the power at His disposal to end the shame. The real miracle of Calvary, as Frederick Buechner once wrote, was that there was no miracle. Yet somehow in that public defeat of His Son, God forged our greatest victory.

Paul described God's amazing strategy this way:

> *God chose the foolish things of the world to shame the wise;*
> *God chose the weak things of the world to shame the strong.*
> *He chose the lowly things of this world and the despised things—*
> *and the things that are not—to nullify the things that are."*

(1 CORINTHIANS 1:27–28)

The onlookers at Golgotha walked home that evening certain that Jesus had been publicly shamed, when, in fact, He had proved all His claims and had won glory.

- *Jesus had overpowered the might of Rome—only He had used weakness to do it.*
- *He had proved invincible before death—only He had used death to conquer death.*
- *He had turned out to be King after all—only He was not like any king who had ever reigned.*

Jesus knew that our hunger for heaven would draw us to Him. Early Christians put a name to that longing— "Christ in you, the hope of glory"

And who was really shamed that day? "Having disarmed the powers and authorities," wrote Paul, "he made a public spectacle of them, triumphing over them at the cross" (Colossians 2:15).

When Jesus prayed that night for His glory to be revealed, He prayed for you and me, too—"for those who will believe in me through [the disciples'] message…. Father, I want those you have given me to be with me where I am, and to see my glory…" (John 17: 20, 24).

Do you hunger to encounter the awesome glory of Jesus? Paul said that the glory awaiting him in Christ's presence put every present suffering in proper perspective. He said that all creation groans in hope of this great unveiling and that we as believers "groan inwardly as we wait eagerly for…the redemption of our bodies" (Romans 8:18, 22–23).

Jesus knew that our hunger for heaven—our sense of incompleteness now and our joy in what is to come—would draw us to Him. It is a famine of His making. Even for Jesus it was not glory in the moment, but the powerful hunger for the glory to come that was at work at the cross. Early Christians put a name to that longing—"Christ in you, the hope of glory" (Colossians 1:27).

As you give Him your shame and weakness today, may He set that hope of glory before you like a feast.

PRAYER

Lord, I praise You for enduring shame for me—
for not reaching for any other kind of miracle.
As I seek to bear my cross for You today, give me Your strength.
Thank You that I never need to be ashamed of the gospel,
"the power of God for the salvation of everyone who believes."
As I wrestle with the hunger You have given me for Yourself,
help me settle for no other, lesser satisfaction.
Someday soon may these very eyes behold Your glory;
may these very ears hear You say, "Well done."
Lord Jesus, I do hunger for Your glory—
to see it and to be enveloped in it.
But sometimes in this world it seems
so distant and so dim to me.
When will You return!
When will I see You come in glory?
Until that day, O Lord, sustain me in this desire.
Hold me in Your hands and feed me with Yourself.

Amen

HE SHED HIS BLOOD
SO I CAN BE WHITE AS SNOW

*Jesus also suffered outside
the city gate to make the people
holy through his own blood.*

HEBREWS 13:12

I can understand how reading about blood, especially for an entire chapter, might repel you. Perhaps you are tempted to close the book here. Let's admit it: We humans react instinctively to that red substance that courses through our veins. When we see someone bleeding, something inside makes us want to run or cry out, "Quick! Do something—this is life or death!"

But talking about blood does not have to be shocking—it can be comforting. Paul, for example, opened his letter to the Ephesians by reminding them of the incredible inheritance that became theirs when Christ shed His blood on the cross:

17

In him we have redemption through his blood,
the forgiveness of sins, in accordance with the riches
of God's grace.

(EPHESIANS 1:7)

Yes, bloodshed is the epitome of violence. But for you and me, blood is also the costly guarantee of a most extravagant gift of grace.

∽

We can't escape the fact that the Bible is a bloodstained book. The word "blood" occurs more than four hundred times in the Old and New Testaments. The first family story after Adam and Eve were cast out of Eden is about brothers, Cain and Abel, whose differences escalated to bloodshed. God brought the murderer, Cain, to task: "What have you done? Listen! Your brother's blood cries out to me from the ground" (Genesis 4:10). That crime was just the beginning. The Old Testament histories often read like collected stories of carnage, murder, and revenge.

Yet it is the religious importance of blood as the symbol of life that is more significant. The law of Moses declared:

For the life of a creature is in the blood,
and I have given it to you to make atonement
for yourselves on the altar; it is the blood that
makes atonement for one's life.

(LEVITICUS 17:11)

For more than a thousand years, Jews fastidiously observed this "no blood" principle in their diet and followed elaborate rules for butchering and draining animals and fowls before they were cooked.

Can you imagine, then, how repulsed and offended His disciples were when Jesus told them flatly, "I tell you the truth, unless you eat the flesh of the Son of Man and drink his blood, you have no life in you" (John 6:53)?

Eat his flesh? Drink his blood? The disciples reeled at the gruesome thought and cult-like associations. "This is a hard teaching," they exclaimed. "Who can accept it?" (John 6:60). John reported that many disciples quit following Jesus on the spot (John 6:66). Still, Jesus refused to explain away the offense.

The closest He ever came to explaining what He meant was on the last night He spent with His disciples. As they lounged around the table sharing their Passover meal, Jesus suddenly reached for the age-old meaning of Passover—and swung it from past to future. On that historic night in Egypt, the shed blood of a lamb had spared the Israelites from death. Now Jesus established a new covenant.

We can't escape the fact that the Bible is a blood-stained book.

He broke apart a loaf of bread, gave thanks, and handed the pieces to them. "This is my body given for you; do this in remembrance of me," He said (Luke 22:19). Then He held up a cup of wine, returned thanks, and passed it around the circle. "Drink from it, all of you," He said. "This is my blood of the covenant, which is poured out for many for the forgiveness of sins" (Matthew 26:27–28).

From then on Jesus' followers were to commemorate the ultimate sacrifice of their Savior, whose shed blood and broken body purchased an eternal atonement. In our communities of faith today, we treasure that celebration as Holy Communion, the Lord's Supper, or the service of the Eucharist.

"Do this in remembrance of me," Jesus said.

And how can we forget? His precious blood still cries out to us.

The love of Jesus washed Golgotha in cardinal hues. Darkening to terracotta, and then to nearly black, His blood left a mark on thorns, iron, wood, and soil. And it stained the hands of His oppressors.

But here is an enduring mystery of the cross: When you kneel there, the dark stains on your hands disappear. By the miracle of grace, the blood of Christ cleanses you completely. "The blood of Jesus…purifies us from all sin," wrote John (1 John 1:7).

According to Revelation, the miracle of Jesus' blood will be one of the grand hymns of eternity:

> *You are worthy. . . because you were slain,*
> *and with your blood you purchased men for God*
> *from every tribe and language and people and nation.*
>
> (REVELATION 5:9)

Even in heaven, Jesus will appear "dressed in a robe dipped in blood" (Revelation 19:13).

But if you have let His blood stain you, you will be as white as snow.

PRAYER

Jesus, You who bled and died for me,
Bring me now to the foot of Your cross.
Let me see Your wounds.
Let me hear the sound of Your blood
crying out to the Father...for me.
By Your grace give me to understand,
as much as I am able, that it was my sin
that brought such violence to You,
and Your love that allowed it.
I fall before You in thanksgiving for
the grace of cleansing through Your blood.
Praise You, my Savior!
Praise You for all You have done!

Amen

HIS HEART WAS PIERCED
SO MINE COULD BE MADE WHOLE

"They will look on me,
the one they have pierced."

ZECHARIAH 12:10

*N*ot many months ago, I thought I felt my heart break. At the time, I was holding the hand of a dying friend, looking into his familiar face, now swollen from chemotherapy, and realizing that I would never see him again in this world. In those moments at his bedside, I realized how much I needed that face, which had given me smiles and encouragement for almost twenty-five years. I confronted again the inescapable reality of death. At the same time, I saw the deep beauty of the order of things and knew that, for a believer, death is really the door to life. So I sat with my friend's frail hand in mine, awed by his great courage. He was showing me, I understood, how a Christian man dies.

18

Though the term is often used, rarely are our hearts truly "broken." The human heart is not as fragile a thing as many imagine. The sight of genuine beauty, if it is unspoiled, can sometimes shatter it. Courage or hearing the truth spoken with conviction can cause a fracture in our easy indifference. Most often, though, it is grief that breaks our heart.

$$\infty$$

The Gospel of John is the only narrative that documents the physical breaking of Jesus' heart.

As we've seen, when the soldiers saw that Jesus had stopped breathing, they realized that they didn't need to break His legs. But Roman law mandated that the soldiers make certain the victim was dead, so one of them took his spear, or *pilum,* and executed the thrust every warrior of the empire was trained to deliver—through the ribs, straight to the heart.

John says that both blood and water came pouring from the wound in Jesus' side (John 19:34). If the wound came from the right side, the blood that flowed from it probably came from the left ventricle of the heart. The "water" was almost certainly the clear fluid from the pericardial sack that surrounds the heart. Some medical experts believe the presence of both fluids together indicate that Jesus' heart may have ruptured, perhaps during the last shout from the cross.

In the next verse, an abrupt and unfamiliar voice breaks into the narrative:

> *The man who saw it has given testimony, and his testimony is true. He knows that he tells the truth, and he testifies so that you also may believe.*

(JOHN 19:35)

John obviously felt an unusual urgency to document his source for this detail. Who was this witness? Was John speaking of himself? Could it have been the same soldier who administered the stabbing? Or could it have been the centurion who had confessed, "Surely this man was the Son of God"? Perhaps he had become a follower of Jesus and had witnessed this scene.

Although we can only speculate about the identity of the witness, John makes absolutely clear the witness's purpose: "He knows that he tells the truth, and he testifies so that you also may believe."

So that you might believe *what?* That Jesus died? That when He was pierced, some combination of bodily fluids flowed from the wound? I don't think so. The answer lies in John's purpose for writing his Gospel: "But these are written *that you may believe* that Jesus is the Christ, the Son of God, and that by believing you may have life in his name" (John 20:31, emphasis added).

"That you may believe...."

Whoever he was, the witness sends his testimony down through the centuries to us so that through our own response of believing, we can receive life in Jesus' name.

Perhaps the witness knew it was true because the sight of it had broken his own heart as dusk fell that day on Golgotha. In the water and the blood that flowed from Jesus' side, he saw the severe beauty of Christ's sacrificial death. In that violence, he encountered—later, if not at the moment—the grace of a new truth: Death could now be defeated by life in His name!

John felt an unusual urgency to document his source for this detail. Who was this witness? Could it have been the centurion who had confessed, "Surely this man was the Son of God"?

What that witness experienced, you too are invited to experience. Today, you can stand at the foot of the cross and let the beauty and courage of our Lord wash over you. You can be broken by grief. You can allow your safe, convenient faith to be cracked open:

> *We considered him stricken by God, smitten by him,*
> *and afflicted. But he was pierced for our transgressions...."*

> (Isaiah 53:4–5)

But I promise you that as you courageously look into Jesus' face, you will be changed. You will become His urgent, passionate witness in this broken world.

And your heart will be made whole.

PRAYER

Lord, I need to be drawn toward Your cross.
Help me watch and wait there.
I need to see the heartbreaking beauty of what You did for me.
I need to understand this truth, which alone sets me free.
I come to You, as always, so full of need.
But, Jesus, it is You, Yourself—more than
any other gift or provision—that I need.
And if it requires that my heart be broken to have You,
then take my heart and break it,
else it will never truly be made whole.

Amen

HE DIED AND WAS BURIED
SO THE GRAVE COULD NOT HOLD ME

Joseph took the body, wrapped it in a clean linen cloth, and placed it in his own new tomb that he had cut out of the rock. He rolled a big stone in front of the entrance to the tomb and went away.

MATTHEW 27:59–60

It is late in the afternoon on the day of preparation for the Passover. A Pharisee appears at the Praetorium with a request for Pilate. His name is Joseph, and he is from the Judean town of Arimathea. He is a man of considerable means and a notable member of the Sanhedrin.

"I am here," Joseph says forthrightly, "to ask for Jesus' body." Jewish law, he reminds the governor, requires that people condemned to death be buried on the same day (Deuteronomy 21:22). *But why,* Pilate wonders, *would someone of this man's standing want to identify himself with a convicted criminal?*

Joseph is a good and upright man. He has been waiting for the kingdom of God and did not consent to the Council's decision. Secretly, he is a disciple of Jesus (John 19:38).

Pilate mulls over his choices. Refusing to allow the burial of Jesus would be a clear statement of political contempt. Besides, the bodies of those crucified were not normally handed over to friends or relatives. Typically, someone in his position would at least demand payment for the body.

But Pilate does none of these things. Perhaps he knows that Joseph was one of the few Council members who hadn't gone along with the majority, and he wants to make it clear that he also thought that Jesus had been wrongly accused and unjustly put to death.

Whatever Pilate's reason, Joseph leaves the governor's residence with official permission to bury Jesus. Immediately, he hastens to Golgotha to claim the body of the dead rabbi.

∽

Imagine the scene at the foot of the cross: The sun is dropping toward the horizon. The crowds have left; the grim entertainment is over. The soldiers are gone, their task accomplished. All three victims hang lifeless and disfigured from their crossbeams. Dogs skulk at the edges.

Still, a somber cluster of women keeps vigil nearby. "In Galilee these women had followed him and cared for his needs," writes Mark. "Many other women who had come up with him to Jerusalem were also there" (Mark 15:41). Mary Magdalene and Salome are there, as is Mary, the mother of Jesus.

The women watch as Joseph sets about the grim task. "Then he took it down," Luke writes (Luke 24:53). With scaffolding or ladders? And how are the massive nails removed? We don't know.

Somehow Joseph—now joined by Nicodemus, another secret follower in the Sanhedrin—tenderly, silently lower the body from the cross.

"Taking Jesus' body," writes John, "the two of them wrapped it, with the spices, in strips of linen. This was in accordance with Jewish burial customs" (John 19:40).

With the women following, the two men carry the wrapped body to a nearby garden cemetery where Joseph owns a tomb "in which no one had ever been laid" (John 19:41). Joseph has provided a new tomb—suitable for royalty. There they stretch Jesus out.

As they finish, dusk is nearly upon them. Nicodemus has brought seventy-five pounds of myrrh and aloes for the burial rite—enough perfume to honor a king. But the Sabbath is about to start. Any further anointing of the body with oils or spices will have to wait until Sunday.

How are the massive nails removed? We don't know. Somehow—tenderly, silently—they lower the body from the cross.

The two men roll a massive stone over the tomb's entrance and leave. Soon the women, too, are gone.

Evening shadows descend upon Golgotha and on the garden. But the corpse of the King of the Jews is already shut up in total darkness.

∞

Most victims of crucifixion, which is to say most criminals, were buried in unmarked graves as a sign of dishonor. Remarkably, Jesus' body was not treated in that fashion. The Gospels are careful to note a series of important details:

- ⤷ *The burial of Jesus was closely observed by a number of witnesses, many of them identified and named.*
- ⤷ *The two men who buried Jesus were well educated, highly respected, and undoubtedly well known in Jerusalem.*
- ⤷ *The location and age of the tomb was described.*
- ⤷ *The women who followed Joseph were reported as seeing the tomb "and how his body was laid in it."*

(LUKE 23:55)

These details are important. Anticipating skeptics who to this day challenge Christ's resurrection, God appears to have taken every precaution to make sure there was clear and irrefutable physical evidence of Christ's death and burial.

Ironically, it was the priests and Pharisees—not Jesus' followers—who "proved" His resurrection. Sometime the next day, the Sabbath, a bad case of nerves brought a number of them back to Pilate's quarters:

> "Sir," they said, "we remember that while he was still alive that deceiver said, 'After three days I will rise again.' So give the order for the tomb to be made secure until the third day. Otherwise, his disciples may come and steal the body and tell the people that he has been raised from the dead. This last deception will be worse than the first."

> "Take a guard," Pilate answered. "Go, make the tomb as secure as you know how." So they went and made the tomb secure by putting a seal on the stone and posting the guard.

(MATTHEW 27: 63–66)

Surely now, the religious leaders thought, *this Jesus debacle has been put to rest.* The soldiers had put an iron point in His heart. Hundreds had seen Him hanging lifeless by the road. Dozens had witnessed His body being lifted from the cross, wound from head to toe in burial cloth, and buried. Men had rolled a heavy stone over the entrance to the tomb. The tomb had been sealed. The seal was being guarded....

Meanwhile in a borrowed tomb, God was keeping His promise.

Finally, the religious leaders could go home and breathe easily.

❧

Meanwhile in the borrowed tomb, God was keeping His promise. "For I am going to do something in your days that you would not believe, even if you were told" (Habakkuk 1:5). "I will ransom them from the power of the grave; I will redeem them from death," he had declared through the prophet Hosea (Hosea 13:14).

In some mysterious way that I don't understand, the tomb during those hours became God's workshop to undo the tragedy of Eden. "You must not eat from the tree of the knowledge of good and evil, for when you eat of it you will surely die," God had warned the first humans (Genesis 2:17). But they hadn't listened. Sin had entered the world through one man's choice, and along with sin came its consequence, death (Romans 5:12).

Only one man—completely just and holy, fully man and fully God—could undo such a disaster. A second Adam. And that one man had just allowed Himself to be brutally executed and buried. Jesus was not unconscious; He was dead. He was not holding out with a last-minute miracle; the last minute had passed. He was not waiting; His will and mind and pulse simply were no more.

But God—His Father and yours and mine—had a plan:

> *For if, by the trespass of the one man, death reigned through that one man, how much more will those who receive God's abundant provision of grace and of the gift of righteousness reign in life through, one man, Jesus Christ.*
>
> (ROMANS 5:17)

Jesus' corpse lay stretched out in that tomb because it was God's will that, in order to pay our ransom, He meet sin and death alone and in the dark.

In those hours, violence reigned absolute, and all creation waited for the Father to make His move.

PRAYER

Jesus, You laid lifeless and sealed in a tomb for three days.
There, by Your death, You gave birth to our hope.
There, in the ultimate defeat that is death,
You won a great victory over death for the whole human race.
Thank You for dying for me.
With Paul, I pray: I want to know You.
I am ready to share in Your sufferings.
I long to become more like You in Your death
and experience the amazing power of Your resurrection.

Amen

HE AROSE AGAIN
SO I MIGHT EXPERIENCE ETERNAL LIFE

> *By his power God raised the Lord from the dead, and he will raise us also.*
>
> 1 CORINTHIANS 6:14

The morning of triumph begins in the quietness of the predawn dark. Mary Magdalene steps out into the chill air and starts walking through the streets of Jerusalem toward Golgotha and the tomb nearby. She comes with spices to anoint the dead body. Since sundown on Friday, she has wanted to be there, just to be near the loved one so violently taken from her. But the Sabbath intervened. Other women disciples rise early, put costly spices in their baskets, and hurry in the same direction (Mark 16:1–2).

20

Mary arrives first. As the first rays of light fill the garden, they fall on the tomb. It yawns open—the stone has been rolled to one side!

Spinning on her heels—rushing past the other women just entering the garden—the frightened and confused Mary breaks into a dash back in the direction she has come. She must tell Peter and John. "They have taken the Lord out of the tomb!" she exclaims when she finds them. "And we don't know where they have put him!" (John 20:2).

Now it is Peter and John's turn to run. John, younger and faster, races ahead of his friend to the tomb. But he stops at the entrance, an obedient Jew. As he hesitates, Peter rushes past him, straight into the tomb.

Mary was right. The body of Jesus is gone. The grave clothes lie in folds, with the cloth that had been wrapped around Jesus' head folded and set aside separately. The fragrance of spices lingers, and that is all.

Peter returns to the city to report his findings, "wondering to himself what had happened" (Luke 24:12). But Mary stays behind, weeping.

Stolen. The body of her Lord has been stolen. Of all the indignities and injuries heaped on their master, this final desecration seems too hard to bear.

Alone in the garden once more, Mary again looks into the tomb. This time, two angels meet her gaze.

"Woman, why are you crying?" one asks.

Startled, Mary replies, "They have taken my Lord away and I don't know where they have put him" (John 20:13).

Sensing a presence behind her, she turns. A man is standing there.

"Woman, why are you crying?" He asks.

In her desperate state, perhaps averting her eyes, puffy with weeping, she mistakes Him for the gardener. "Sir," she pleads, "if you have carried him away, tell me where you have put him, and I will get him" (John 20:15).

Then the man calls her by name: "Mary…"

"My Rabbi!" she cries, and with unspeakable joy, she falls before Him, her arms reaching involuntarily around His nail-marked feet.

∽◯◠

It is hard for me to imagine Jesus' tone of voice other than touched with quiet laughter.

"Mary...."

Just the sound of her name spoken by the Master began Mary's own resurrection story. Jesus was not stolen, but risen. And He had risen for her.

The stories of Mary and the others who personally encountered Jesus on Resurrection morning are among the all-time favorites for Christians. These stories speak to us of hope, of new beginnings, of victory over tears and disappointment, of eventual triumph over death, and of joy. Most of all, they remind of us of who we are: We belong to Him, and He to us. We are the people of Resurrection morning, when new life in Christ prevailed over violence, and the age of amazing grace began.

But have you ever noticed how quietly the grace of Easter arrived? No angelic choirs heralded Jesus' return from the grave. No foreign dignitaries arrived bearing gifts. No voice thundered from heaven.

The sounds of the Resurrection are different. They are much more personal:

- *muffled voices at dawn, the sound of sandals passing in the streets;*
- *her name hanging in the morning air, and Mary's gasp of recognition;*

- Peter and John whispering as they hurry back to town—wondering, hoping, wanting so much to believe;
- three men walking together toward Emmaus, talking quietly among themselves—two heartbroken at the death of a dream, the third trying to restore their hope;
- ten hushed disciples waiting in the upper room—fearful, uncertain what to do next, when Jesus appears in their midst and says, "Peace be with you."

After all the public pronouncements at Jesus' birth, the tumult of His life, and the public horror of His death, I must confess that I like the peace and quiet of Easter Morning. The Resurrection unfolds entirely in a series of intimate conversations between Jesus and His followers. It's all family business. As He did with Mary, Jesus rises for each of us and calls us by name. The promise is for everyone, but the experience of Easter is only for those who believe and have longed for His appearing.

When we least expect it, our risen Lord comes to us.

The violence of Easter is a quiet one, too—but more far-reaching and destructive than any that preceded it or that could ever follow.

The tables have been turned. Now violence does not fall upon Jesus. Instead, because God raised Him from the grave, Jesus is the one who delivers a devastating blow to the kingdom of darkness. The violence of the Resurrection, says Paul, is nothing less than the death of death:

> *Grace…has now been revealed through the appearing of our*

Savior, Christ Jesus, who has destroyed death and has brought life and immortality to light through the gospel.

(2 TIMOTHY 1:9–10)

When we least expect it, our risen Lord comes to us. "I *am* the resurrection and the life," he tells us (John 11:25, emphasis added). Then He invites us to share in His resurrection power and take upon ourselves His righteousness so that we can stand confidently in the presence of the Father.

"I am the Living One," He says to us. "I was dead, and behold I am alive for ever and ever! And I hold the keys to death and Hades" (Revelation 1:18).

And in a gentle voice, He speaks our name.

PRAYER

Loving Father, thank You for bringing Jesus back
from the grave for me.
Thank You for conquering death and darkness by Your power.
You knew how desperately I needed to be rescued.
My praise and thanks and worship, my God, belong to You!
You are the God who saves. You are the God who lives in me
and gives life to all Your children through Your Spirit.
And thank You, Risen and Conquering Savior—
thank You for Your love and for Your gift of new life.
Thank You for coming to find me.
You call me by name still, and I follow.
Oh, please help me to hear and follow always!

Amen.

HE IS KNOWN BY HIS SCARS
SO I WILL TAKE UP MY CROSS
AND FOLLOW HIM

> *We always carry around in our body*
> *the death of Jesus, so that the life of Jesus*
> *may also be revealed in our body.*

2 CORINTHIANS 4:10

*W*hat does the resurrected life look like?

Jesus walked out of the grave looking different somehow. He was still the rabbi from Nazareth; He still had a physical body; and His voice sounded the same. But at first even His close friends were not certain that it was really Him.

Jesus chose to reveal Himself by His scars. In a succession of appearances to His disciples, He showed them His hands, His feet, and His side (John 20:20, 27).

21

"Why do doubts rise in your minds?" He asked them when they thought He was a ghost. "Look at my hands and my feet. It is I myself!" (Luke 24:39).

Have you ever wondered why the Father chose not to erase those marks of humiliation from the Son's otherwise perfect resurrection body? After all, God's power had overcome all the violence—long hours of suffering, a spear to the heart, and death itself. Why not remove the reminders of Christ's injuries? Why have the wounded Messiah, the crucified King, carry His scars into eternity?

I believe the answer is found in the final act of violent grace.

This violence is not like the ones that fell on Jesus—those ended with His death on the cross. Neither is it like the violence that occurred when Jesus destroyed death—that was accomplished by God's power when Jesus walked out of the tomb.

The final violence is an invitation from the Crucified One to a crucifixion. And the crucifixion is ours.

⁂

Jesus had broken the hard news about the crucified life to His disciples immediately after Peter made his breakthrough realization—"You are the Christ, the Son of the living God" (Matthew 16:16). Jesus responded to Peter's testimony by telling His disciples how He was going to build His church. Great days seemed ahead.

But it was not the kind of success that Peter and the others had envisioned. "From that time on Jesus began to explain to his disciples that he must go to Jerusalem and suffer many things," writes Matthew. When Peter strongly objected, Jesus chastised him. "You do not have in mind the things of God," He said, "but the things of men" (Matthew 16:21, 23).

Then Jesus tenderly, firmly revealed what "the things of God" would look like in their lives:

> *If anyone would come after me, he must deny himself*
> *and take up his cross and follow me. For whoever*

> *wants to save his life will lose it, but whoever loses*
> *his life for me will find it.*

(MATTHEW 16:24–25)

The simple fact is, if we take the name "Christian," we, too, must be recognized by our scars. The visible proofs of crucifixion—not our accomplishments, degrees, possessions, or wealth—will become our identifying marks.

That is the only kind of kingdom of which Jesus is King! And all the disciples who heard Him that day would take up their own crosses, receive their own scars on this earth, and, with the exception of one, die for love of their Lord.

∽∾

What does the resurrected life look like?

Jesus thought it looked something like breakfast on the beach. Though he was now the King of Glory, one morning Jesus went to the shore of the Sea of Galilee to prepare breakfast for His disciples. Peter and six ohters had been in the boat all night, fishing. When they confessed that they hadn't caught anything, Jesus told them where to cast their nets. Soon they were dragging an enormous catch onto the beach.

> *If we take the name "Christian," the visible proofs of crucifixion will become our identifying marks.*

And there was the risen Lord. Jesus had made a fire, cleaned several fish, prepared bread, and was waiting patiently for them to return to shore.

Do you see the miracle? The catch of fish is just a detail. The real wonder is that the resurrected Lord was serving these weak, unreliable, unpromising men. The one who had fed them, cared for their needs, and washed their feet before His death was now fixing their breakfast. At the heart of His glory is servanthood, the true mark of the crucified life.

Jesus died a slave's death on the cross, not so He could somehow later "lord it over" His disciples. He suffered to serve. He endured the humiliation because that is what servants do.

Do you wonder where to begin today to follow in the steps of the Lord of Grace? The crucified life begins in servanthood:

> *And being found in appearance as a man,*
> *he humbled himself and became obedient to death—*
> *even death on a cross!*
>
> (Philippians 2:8)

I must warn you that, when we take them as chosen marks of our life, humility and obedience to Christ threaten to change us completely. They will do violence to the old, selfish, superficially promising pursuits that we have mistaken for life. "We always carry around in our body the death of Jesus," wrote Paul, "so that the life of Jesus may also be revealed in our body (2 Corinthians 4:10).

Out of the beautiful violence of His life will flow a river of grace that will change our world.

To stand before the cross is to give yourself to Scripture and prayer in order to "be there" as only the Word and Spirit can enable you to do. To do this work is to be filled with amazement.

For the believer, grace means Gods' Riches At Christ's

Expense. Until we embrace this costly grace—or rather until we allow ourselves to be embraced by it—we can never know what it means to be completely accepted. Never experience a deep sense of unqualified adoption as a daughter or son. Never realize what it is to really live. Never be moved to take up our own cross each day and follow Him.

I pray that this book has helped you rediscover some of your original passion and purpose in following Christ. I hope that you have experienced a new awareness of what God's gentle violence and surpassing grace can accomplish in your life. This has been my experience in the writing of it.

On one hand, the cross is a mirror held up to my sin that shows me, through the price that was paid, just how thoroughly lost I am:

> *For the wages of sin is death,*
> *but the gift of God is eternal life*
> *in Christ Jesus our Lord.*
>
> (ROMANS 6:23)

On the other hand, the cross is a window held up to my Lord that shows me how greatly loved I am:

> *Greater love has no one than this,*
> *that he lay down his life for his friends.*
>
> (JOHN 15:13)

The cross of Jesus gives the gift of that great love to you and to me.

And there is no greater love.

PRAYER

Lord, we see the scars on Your hands and feet and side.
We know how they got there,
and most especially, we know why they got there.
We are the ones who wounded You;
we drove in the nails and spear.
Look upon our repentance, O Lord,
see the sorrow for our sins and remember we belong now to You.
Praise You, Lord, for Your infinite riches of grace
poured out upon us at Calvary.
Give us the courage to stand fast for You,
to take up the cross of our love, even when it means scars and tears,
even if it means death for Your sake.
For this is our eternal joy and salvation, to know You,
our crucified and risen Lord.

Amen